*Reading* ZEN *in the Rocks*

*François Berthier*

*Reading* ZEN *in the Rocks*

THE JAPANESE DRY LANDSCAPE GARDEN

*Translated and with a Philosophical Essay by Graham Parkes*

THE UNIVERSITY OF CHICAGO PRESS • CHICAGO AND LONDON

François Berthier is professor of Japanese art and history at the Institut Nationale des Langues et Civilizations Orientales in Paris.

Graham Parkes is professor of philosophy at the University of Hawaii.

Originally published as *Le jardin du Ryōanji: Lire le Zen dans les pierres,* © 1989, 1997 Société Nouvelle Adam Biro

The University of Chicago Press, Chicago 60637
The University of Chicago Press, Ltd., London
© 2000 by The University of Chicago
All rights reserved. Published 2000
Printed in the United States of America

09 08 07 06 05 04 03 02 01 00    1 2 3 4 5

Photo Credits: frontispiece, 8, 28, 29: Édouard Boubat/Top; 1: courtesy of the Freer Gallery of Art, Smithsonian Institution, Washington, D.C.; 5: Idemitsu Museum of Arts, Tokyo; 13: Inge Morath/Magnum; 14: Toni Schneiders/Rapho; 15: Jean-Philippe Charbonnier/Top; 20: Pan-Asia Photo News/Rapho; 25: Frédéric Rapho; 26: René Burri/Magnum; 34: Else Madelon Hooykaas/Rapho

ISBN: 0-226-04411-4 (cloth)

Library of Congress Cataloging-in-Publication Data
Berthier, François.
    [Jardin du Ryōanji. English]
    Reading Zen in the rocks : the Japanese dry landscape garden / François Berthier ; translated and with a philosophical essay by Graham Parkes.
        p. cm.
    Includes bibliographical references (p. ) and index.
    ISBN 0-226-04411-4 (cloth)
    1. Rock gardens, Japanese—Zen influences.   2. Rock gardens—Japan—Kyoto.   3. Ryōanji Teien (Kyoto, Japan).   I. Parkes, Graham, 1949–  II. Title.
    SB458.B4713 2000
    712'.6'0952—dc21                                                      99-043678

CONTENTS

# TRANSLATOR'S PREFACE

To begin at the end, on the back cover of the French original of François Berthier's book on the Japanese "dry landscape" garden:

Is there a language of stone? A few unhewn rocks distributed on an expanse of gravel—could they be delivering a message? This is ultimately the question posed by the garden at Ryōanji in Kyoto. This garden is disconcerting through its not really being a garden: there is no green of trees to be seen, no scent of flowers to be caught, nor any birdsong to be heard. This desertlike space is enigmatic, an arid area where just fifteen rocks measure themselves against the immensity of the void. Five centuries old, the garden of Ryōanji is a surprisingly modern work of art. It is also a place where the human being can read, in the dark mirror of stone, the mystery that he carries within.[1]

These are provocative suggestions, for we don't normally think of rocks as having language, nor of gardens devoid of vegetation as posing questions, nor of stone as something that can be read, and possessing surfaces reflecting something in the depths of human being. But rock and stone in the Japanese dry landscape garden are and do just these things.

A brief word first on the distinction between "stone" and "rock": both terms are mass nouns (as in "outcrop of rock" or "staircase of stone") as well as singular nouns ("a precious stone," "a strangely shaped rock"), and they are often used interchangeably. Although rocks are originally found in nature, unlike stones they remain rocks when moved into a garden. (We speak of "rock gardens" rather than "stone gardens.") "Rock" generally retains a connotation of naturalness by comparison with "stone," insofar as we talk sooner of stone as being worked—or else unhewn—and at the extreme of being worked we call them "precious stones" (which unfortunately, in the case of diamonds, are colloquially referred to as "rocks"). "Rocks" are in general larger than "stones," and in Japanese gardens it is usually the larger components that draw our attention. Although Professor Berthier writes almost exclusively of *pierres* and only occasionally of *rocs,* I have rendered both terms mostly as "rocks" in the belief that this is more consonant with English usage.

Japanese studies in the West have often been intoxicated by exoticism, to the point of uncritical adulation of their subject, while the corresponding field in Japan has frequently taken the form of *Nihonjinron,* beginning as discussions of what it means to be Japanese but then degenerating into "theories of Japanese uniqueness." Some of the writing on Japanese gardens has tended to overemphasize their uniqueness in terms of generalized oppositions of the "Western gardens are this" versus "Japanese gardens are not-this" variety. But recent scholarship on Japan in the United States has sometimes overreacted to the silliness of the *Nihonjinron* literature by claiming that in fact the Japanese aren't as different from us as they like to think, thereby dissolving all cultural practices (and corresponding discourses) into a flat postmodernist melange of *indifférance*. There is a danger here in overlooking what is genuinely different about Japanese culture, which makes it eminently worth studying.

The history of the Japanese garden is, as Berthier's text suggests, a long and complex one, and the reflections that follow concern only those aspects that will enhance our appreciation of the *karesansui* (dry landscape) style in particular. Since stone has in general been understood differently in the Western traditions from the way it has been regarded in East Asia, a focus on the role of rock in these cultures may be especially helpful for the foreign viewer of—or reflector upon—such gardens. My complementary essay pursues Berthier's suggestion that stone speaks to us, by asking what kind of voice rocks may have and what they might be saying. Histories of Japanese garden making naturally acknowledge the influences of Chinese ideas and practices on the development of the art in Japan, but it is beyond the scope of Berthier's project to treat this topic at any length. However, since the Japanese understanding of stone is more or less continuous with the Chinese, and since Chinese culture manifests a petromania—not to mention litholatry—unparalleled in any other (except Japanese), I have seen fit to treat this distinctively East Asian understanding at some length.

In the context of the Japanese dry landscape garden (and its prototypes in China) the focus is on stone revered for its own sake, for the pleasure and understanding derived from simply being in the presence of rocks and contemplating them, rather than for their usefulness as tools or raw material, their medicinal value as minerals, their role in alchemical practices, or their worth as precious stones. In this respect there is little in the Western tradition to compare with the traditional reverence for stone in Chinese and Japanese culture. Nor have more than a few thinkers in Europe or America deemed unhewn stone worthy of philosophical reflection. The rare exceptions will be worth a brief discussion, since attitudes toward rock turn out to serve as a kind of touchstone on a point of significant cultural difference.

The ground of this cultural difference appears to lie in the traditional Western dichotomy between the animate and inanimate realms, which has no counterpart in the East Asian traditions. Aesthetic appreciation in China and Japan thus has a greater range than in the West, insofar as it extends to (what we call) "inanimate" matter in art—works that have not been worked by the artist's hand. But the revisioning of our conception of stone that is prompted by contemplation of East Asian rock gardens has implications that go beyond the aesthetic to the ecological. Any shift in our thinking that weakens anthropocentrism is likely to have beneficial consequences for the natural environment, so that contemporary movements such as "deep ecology" advocate biocentrism as a salutary antidote to human domination and exploitation of nature. But the respect for rock on the part of East Asian makers and connoisseurs of dry landscape gardens, and that is exemplified in the Daoist and Buddhist philosophies underlying the art of garden making, makes biocentrism look narrow and parochial by contrast.

Names are given in the Japanese order, which is usually the family name followed by the given name. In the captions for the photographs, and sometimes elsewhere, I have added the word "temple" to the Japanese temple names, even though those names already contain the word: for example, "Shōjūji Temple" (where *ji* means "temple"). This verges on the solecism committed by saying "Mount Fujisan" (which means "Mount Fuji Mountain"), but is worth risking for purposes of clarity.

I am grateful to William R. LaFleur, who read the entire manuscript for the Press, for providing several most helpful comments and suggestions. A trip to Japan for the purpose of contemplating some examples of the dry landscape garden was supported by a research award from the University of Hawaii Japan Studies Endowment, funded by a grant from the Japanese government.

## Zen and the Arts

I speak of naked stones ... in which there is both concealed and
revealed a mystery that is slower, more vast, and heavier than the
destiny of a transitory space.

ROGER CAILLOIS

Zen is not, properly speaking, a religion: it is one of a dozen
or so main branches of Buddhism. Nor is Zen a philosophy,
at least not in the sense in which the Greeks understood it,
or in the sense the Germans did. Zen is rather a form of
thought, or, better, a mode of thinking that gives rise to a
certain way of acting.

One of the original traits of this branch of Buddhism is

*1* Hermit on the toilet, *a Daoist character. Ink on paper. By Soga Shōhaku, second half of the eighteenth century. Freer Gallery of Art, Smithsonian Institution, Washington, D.C.*

that it is nourished by the sap of Daoism. The primary aim of this ancient Chinese religion is to liberate the human being from the shackles of the rules and conventions imposed by society, and to allow one to regain the marvelous spontaneity of the child, or one's primary nature, original being, or essence (see fig. 1). This project is connected with that of the Zen adept, who is in search of his deepest self.

The basic principle of Zen is very simple: according to Buddhist teaching every creature harbors within it "Buddha-nature"—an expression equivalent to the Christian notion of a "fragment of the divine" or, in terms of Indian thought, to a spark from the great universal fire from which everything emanates and to which everything returns. The human being is, however, unaware of this, and that is precisely where the difficulties begin. How can one become aware of this "Buddha-nature" that is buried in one's inner-most depths? To do this, to attain enlightenment, all methods are fine, including the most extravagant. The path that the Zen monk usually follows is threefold: it includes disconcerting conversations with the master, long periods of sitting meditation, and long stretches of manual activity—since one must practice with the body as well as with the mind.

The men that forged Zen in China between the sixth and seventh centuries were eccentrics, and indeed quite disputatious types (figs. 2 and 3). Art was one of the things they called into question; some of them were even iconoclasts. A similar attitude is to be found in Japan when Zen took root there in the thirteenth century. Up to the Muromachi period (1338–1573) Buddhist art in Japan consisted mainly of sculpture and painting. But since they had little appreciation for idolatry, the Zen monks had little respect for religious images. They regarded worship of objects and recitation of sutras for them as quite superficial activities that failed to engage one's entire being. In the realm of art they privileged the garden most of all as a means of expression. What dictated this choice?

In his *Dream Dialogues,* Musō Soseki wrote: "He who distinguishes between the garden and practice cannot be said to have found the true Way." What the great monk meant was that to create a garden is a way of practicing Zen. Such an assertion implies close connections between the art of the garden and the search for truth.

In the gardens of the Heian period (794–1185) all available elements were put to work: trees, grasses and flowers, sand, rocks, and water. Even birds and fish contributed to the composition. There was also a preference for deciduous

2 Huineng, Sixth Patriarch of Zen, *tearing up sutras. Ink on paper. By Liangkai, thirteenth century.*

trees, whose shapes and colors would vary with the changing seasons: their flowers would blossom in spring, their foliage become green in the summer and then red in autumn, and their branches grow bare in winter. Thanks to the eternal cycle of the seasons, these gardens would exemplify the Buddhist teaching of the incessant cycle of death and rebirth, while also displaying the ephemeral character of this world in which everything continually changes.

The Zen gardens of the Muromachi period stem from a quite different conception. One of their characteristics is a strict limitation on the kinds of materials used: they consist mainly of rocks and sand, with only occasional vegetation in the form of evergreen bushes that grow slowly, so that these almost unchanging gardens seem to be somehow anchored in time. The gardens of the Heian period reflected the vicissitudes of human life, whereas the Zen monks rejected transitory phenomena and worthless appearances. They stripped nature bare in order to reveal its substance: their "bare bones" gardens expressed universal essence.

According to Zen it is impossible to attain supreme consciousness by studying this or that doctrine analytically: one must proceed in a direct and intuitive manner. This is the meaning of a maxim attributed to Huike, the Second Patriarch of Zen: "Pointing directly to the human heart, to grasp one's original nature and so attain enlightenment." One can also "attain enlightenment"—apprehend ultimate truth—through the mediation of natural phenomena. It is then a matter of stripping nature of its skin, of removing from it everything that can be removed. By reducing nature

3 Hanshan, *Zen monk from the seventh to eighth centuries. An impenitent practical joker, but also an inspired poet, he let his hair grow as a sign of rebellion. Colors on silk. Attributed to Yanhui, fourteenth century. National Museum of Tokyo.*

to its smallest dimensions and bringing it back to its simplest expression, one can extract its essence. And it is by seizing the essence of nature that the human being can discover his own "original nature." That is why the Zen monks stripped nature bare, retaining only rocks and sand, and a little vegetation. In this way the gardens they created provided an image of the universe in its most condensed form, in which they were able to discern their own true faces.

6

4 Calabash and Catfish. *Ink and light colors on paper. By Josetsu, circa 1413. Taizō-in, Myōshinji Temple, Kyoto.*

These gardens also played a role in Zen practice. One of the means employed by Zen masters to remove the scales from the eyes of their disciples is the *kōan,* an apparently nonsensical puzzle that can only be solved by way of the absurd. There were also pictorial *kōan,* like the one painted by the monk Josetsu on the theme, "How to catch a catfish with a gourd?" (figs. 4 and 5). Correspondingly, certain gardens are *kōan* in three dimensions. The garden of

5 Kōan (*Zen puzzle*). *Ink on paper. By Sengai, first half of the nineteenth century. Idemitsu Museum, Tokyo.*

Ryōanji, about which so much has been written, is as enigmatic as a Zen riddle.

Under the influence of Zen, art from the Muromachi period on tended to become more secular: Buddhist sculpture and painting went into decline. The Chinese monk and painter Mu Qi illustrated this process by creating, in the thirteenth century, an astonishing triptych: while the central image depicts the Bodhisattva Avalokiteshvara (Jpn., Kannon), the two side panels do not even show figures from the Buddhist pantheon but rather depict a crane and a monkey. This has nothing to do with sacrilege, but is rather a lesson on which to meditate.

There is, to be sure, Zen painting and statuary, but these works do not have as their themes buddhas and bodhisattvas: they are rather (imaginary) portraits of the founders of schools (fig. 6) and the great monks of the past, or else (realistic) portraits of contemporary masters (fig. 7). In this way the center of gravity moved from the divine toward the human. In the same movement, the gardens of the Buddha became the gardens of human beings—a new genre of garden exemplifying this kind of austere humanism that characterizes Zen.

The rock gardens also reflected the influence of Song dynasty landscape painting. This sober and lapidary art, which renounced the marvels of color, was a response to the demands of simplicity and austerity that informed the life of the Zen monk. This is what inspired the creators of gardens. According to an ancient master, the temple gardens

6 Bodhidharma, *semi-legendary founder of Zen. Ink on paper. By Hakuin, 1751. Shōjūji Temple, Toyohashi, Aichi Prefecture.*

7 Musō Soseki. *Colors on silk. By Mutō Shūi, 1349. Myōchi-in, Tenryūji Temple, Kyoto.*

are paintings painted without brushes, sutras written without [Chinese] characters.

The rock gardens are a concrete expression of Zen thought, which is not itself accessible to ordinary people. For that reason they appear impenetrable. They are very different from the garden paradises of the Heian period; there is nothing charming about them. On the contrary, they evoke the aridity of the desert, though without its sterility. For the masters animated these rocks in order to nourish the spirits of those in search of their hidden being.[1] In short, it is as difficult to understand Zen gardens as it is to understand one's own self (fig. 8).

### The Beginnings of the Rock Garden

The art of gardens in Japan goes back at least to the fifth century CE: the *Nihonshoki* (Chronicles of Japan) compiled in 720 reports that the Emperor Richū and his wife loved relaxing in a boat on a pond filled

*8 Monk meditating in front of a Zen garden.*

with carp. This is the first written mention of a Japanese garden. Archeological investigations have shown that gardens from the Asuka period (538–645) also included ponds. Other excavations undertaken in Nara, which was the capital of Japan from 710 to 784, show that as early as the eighth century gardens with water already looked in certain respects like Heian-period gardens: a winding stream, a pond of irregular shape with an island in the middle, and groupings of rocks. What is more, the remains of a garden situated within the perimeter of the Imperial Palace in Nara turned out to contain an arrangement of rocks in the style of "dry landscape," which is characteristic of Zen gardens from the Muromachi period.

In antiquity the word for "garden" was *shima,* meaning "island." Situated in an expanse of water, the island would constitute the heart of the garden. It did not have a merely decorative function, but also possessed a symbolic meaning.

Under the influence of Daoism the Chinese of ancient times believed that somewhere in the ocean there floated three or five mountainous islands covered with forests of pearls and coral, filled with birds and animals of dazzling white, and inhabited by fairies and hermits that knew neither old age nor death. Human beings hardy enough to voyage as far as these mysterious islands were said to have attained the secret of unfading youth and eternal life. But instead of searching the seas in order to discover the inaccessible lands of youth and immortality, the Chinese emperor Wudi (156–87 BCE) had rocky islands placed in the pond of his garden.

Belief in these Daoist paradises in Japan is attested from the fifth century on, in the form of a story familiar to every Japanese child to this day: a young fisherman named Urashima Tarō saves the life of a sea turtle. In gratitude the turtle takes him to one of these fantastic islands. There the young man marries a beautiful princess, whereupon time stands still. But when, eventually overcome with homesickness, he forms the desire to see his village again and goes back among human beings, he immediately becomes old and dies.

Since these marine mountains floated and drifted in the ocean, the Emperor of Heaven ordained that turtles should act as pillars in order to stabilize them and keep them still. This is what is behind the appearance of the turtle in the story of Urashima Tarō. But it explains above all why these Daoist lands gave birth, in Japanese gardens, to the "turtle island," which is a kind of substitute for the animal and is traditionally paired with the "crane island"—both creatures being symbols of longevity.

In Japan the best known of the Isles of the Immortals is Hōrai, a common motif in Japanese gardens. But this theme was in competition with that of Mount Sumeru, which, according to the Buddhist conception of the cosmos, rises from the center of the world, surrounded by nine other mountains separated from it by eight seas. A fantastic land, Sumeru is clothed in fragrant trees; at its summit is the palace of Indra, king of the Hindu pantheon; on its slopes are stationed the Four Celestial Kings who guard the four cardinal points.

According to the *Nihonshoki,* a Korean dug a pond in

the garden of the Empress Suiko and erected there a rock depicting Mount Sumeru. Thus from the beginning one sees fused, in a thematic plan, a mythical image from Daoism and a cosmic image from Buddhism, and beyond that from Hinduism. This means that the Japanese garden was informed by the greatest religious currents of East Asia.

After the capital was transferred to Heian-kyō (Kyoto) in 794, a new kind of garden appeared in the Imperial Palace and in the houses of the nobles, even though it was based on the conception of the "Islands" of the seventh and eighth centuries. The residences of the Heian period were built in an architectural style called *shinden-zukuri,* which is distinguished by, among other things, symmetry in the arrangement of its various elements. At the center, the main house (*shinden*) faces south and is flanked by a pavilion to the east and the west, with a third one, to the north in back, completing the arrangement. All these constructions are connected to each other by way of covered galleries. In front of the central building, to the south, is a small square strewn with white sand. This area derives from the sacred precincts of Shinto shrines and the ceremonial esplanade of imperial palaces. Farther to the south is the pond, fed by a winding stream and furnished with one or more rocky islands that are accessible by way of arched culverts. All this is similar to gardens created earlier, but there is nevertheless a notable difference. Formerly every element of the garden was independent, but now the space is unified according to a theme: the aim is to reproduce a site famous for its beauty or some bucolic landscape in the environs of the town.[2] In this way everything conduces to the composition of a tableau, in the manner of *Yamato-e* (Japanese painting).

In the ninth century the Japanese broke off the relations that they had enjoyed with China for more than two centuries and, enriched by everything they had learned from their continental neighbor, devoted themselves to the task of developing their own culture. This step was taken in the realm of painting as well as in that of literature. The new pictorial style that arose in the course of the ninth century was called *Yamato-e*. The artists abandoned Chinese themes in order to paint the landscapes that lay before their eyes. It was natural for this movement to have repercussions that affected the making of gardens, since these tended to represent Japanese landscapes. It is thus easy to understand that certain painters from this period were also garden makers. This was the case with Kose no Kanaoka, a famous court painter, and also with Kose no Hirotaka, one of the masters of *Yamato-e*.

Daoist thought exerted a powerful influence on the Japanese garden. Beyond the idea of the Islands of Immortality, the belief in the four divine animals that reside at the cardinal points of the compass had a profound effect on the organization of space. In the east the Green Dragon rules over moving waters; in the south the Red Phoenix flies over the lowlands; in the west the White Tiger governs the great highways; and in the north the Black Warrior (a tortoise with a serpent coiled around it) reigns over the heights. This conception of space determined the layout of cities as well as the residences of the living and the dead. According to these topographical principles, a garden must have a stream in the east, a depression in the south, a path in the west, and a mountain in the north. If these conditions are satisfied, the four divinities are present and ensure the protection of the place, thereby guaranteeing happiness, health, and long life. But finding a terrain that would satisfy these demands was difficult. Thus three cypresses planted in the north would make up for the lack of a hill, and seven maples set in the west could substitute for the path. (The path would serve the function of diverting to the outside evil spirits that infest the north, an especially ill-omened direction.) Then all that remained was to put in a stream flowing from the east to the southwest, and to dig a pond in the south.

Whether in the form of a spring, a waterfall, a stream, or a pond, water was the dominant element in the pleasure gardens of Japan. Kyoto, a city surrounded on three sides by mountains, suffers from oppressive heat during the summer, and running or still water helps, however little, to temper the stifling heat. One would be refreshed by the sound of small waterfalls and the crystalline murmur of streams. People would go boating in covered skiffs or, sitting by the edge of the pond, would enjoy music issuing from two boats whose prows were graced in one case by the head of a dragon, and in the other by a phoenix with outstretched wings. The pond would be further enlivened by the presence of carp and ducks, and when night fell fireflies and singing insects would be released.

In parallel to the pleasure gardens there appeared religious gardens. The Esoteric School of Shingon Buddhism was the first to set the impress of Buddhist thought on the art of the garden. The monks of this school have a special vision of the spiritual world, which they translate into the form of mandalas, which are, so to speak, cosmic diagrams. In a Shingon monastery the arrangements of the various buildings, as well as of the statues of buddhas and cult objects, are based on the structure of the mandala. There are variations, but the mandala basically has a geometric structure. In the center of the universe is the supreme Buddha Mahavairochana (Dainichi in Japanese), surrounded by a multitude of buddhas set in quadrilateral compartments. But when Shingon monks were creating a garden, it was the spirit of the mandala that they tried to embody, rather than its form, since geometry entails symmetry. Symmetry is not a feature of the Japanese garden, which is rather characterized by a systematic asymmetry. The mandala-gardens were thus highly symbolic. For example, three rocks grouped together would suggest a Buddhist triad; a waterfall was regarded as a manifestation of Achala (Fudō in Japanese), a central figure in the esoteric pantheon who was associated with the waterfalls beneath which ascetics would purify themselves; and the so-called "rocks of the two worlds" referred to Shingon cosmology.[3]

The gardens that derived the most from the contribution of Buddhism were those that evoked the paradise of Amida. This Buddha occupies a special place in the Buddhist pantheon insofar as he is a savior. If a person on the verge of death simply invokes Amida, the Buddha will descend to earth in order to transport the soul of the deceased to the Pure Land over which he reigns. The soul is wrapped in a lotus that is replanted in a magical pond, and when the flower opens the deceased is reborn in Paradise.

The anxiety occasioned by belief in the "Dharma-ending period" increased again in the course of the twelfth century, a time when civil wars raged throughout the country.[4] With this an awareness of the precariousness of life awakened, the recognition of the fragility of human being, and of the ephemerality of all things. This sentiment appeared in the gardens of this era. It is one of the reasons people were especially sensitive to the poignant beauty of spring flowers, which wither quickly or fall from the branch, and to the moving splendor of leaves, which, having flared into vibrant color, die with the advent of winter. The changes undergone by nature in the course of the seasons evoked, in a poetic mode, the impermanence of this world, where nothing abides. In this river in which everything drifts away, the only thing remaining is the hope of gaining entrance to the Paradise of Amida. And while waiting to leave behind this "unclean world" in order to enjoy beatitude in the bosom of the Pure Land, the nobles represented this Pure Land in their gardens, in order to revere the Savior and forget the vicissitudes of earthly life by tasting celestial happiness in advance.

The oldest known paradisal garden was at Byōdō-in near Kyoto, which was originally the country residence of Fujiwara no Yorimichi. In 1052, influenced by belief in the "Dharma-ending period," this statesman decided to transform his villa into a temple consecrated to Amida. Formally speaking, there was little difference between "paradisal" and pleasure gardens. Moreover, the sanctuary of Byōdō-in was conceived in the architectural style of *shinden-zukuri,* which is fundamentally secular. Nevertheless, these types differ perceptibly on the level of signification. For example, in the paradisal garden the pond symbolizes the lotus pond of the Pure Land where the dead are reborn, whereas in the pleasure garden it simply represents the sea or a large lake. The paradisal garden is filled with Buddhist allusions, while the pleasure garden figuratively reconstitutes some natural site. However, the two kinds of garden gradually came to interfuse one another. In the Heian period a number of temples were private institutions, in which the founders sometimes established their residences within the sacred precinct. Or, as in the case of Byōdō-in, the residence was converted into a temple by the owner. In actuality the distinction between the religious and the secular was often not clearly made, a tendency that would become stronger in the Muromachi period.

Although the gardens of the Heian period were essentially water gardens, there already existed at that time "dry landscapes" (*karesansui*), areas without water. The term *karesansui* appears for the first time in the eleventh century in the *Sakuteiki,* the oldest treatise of the art of gardens in Japan. Its author defines "dry landscape" as follows: "a place without a pond or a stream, where one arranges rocks." These gardens were above all descriptive: they reproduced natural sites where there was no sea or lake or river—hence the name "dry landscapes." It is on this technique several centuries old that most Zen gardens were based. At any rate, these latter offered a considerable innovation: they represent landscapes with water without actually using water.

The ancestor of the dry landscape garden in the Zen style is to be found at Saihōji, and was created between 1339 and 1344 by Musō Soseki, a great Zen monk and one of the most eminent garden makers in Japan. He first studied the esoteric teachings of Shingon, but then, attracted by the plain simplicity of Zen, entered the monastery of Kenninji in 1294 at the age of nineteen. The earliest document to mention a garden in his style dates from 1312. Shortly after that, Musō worked at Eihōji Temple in the province of Mino. Then he founded Zuisenji at Kamakura. Eventually he created his two masterpieces, the gardens at Saihōji and Tenryūji in Kyoto. Musō Soseki was the father of the Zen rock garden, and his contributions to the art of the garden in Japan are considerable.

Saihōji, which is better known by its modern name, Kokedera ("Moss Temple"), is situated in the hills that border Kyoto to the west. This temple, which was originally dedicated to Amida, fell into disrepair at the beginning of the fourteenth century. In 1339 a powerful retainer of the Shogun Ashikaga entrusted Musō Soseki with the task of restoring Saihōji and making it into a Zen monastery. The monk gladly accepted this commission, since the hilly site of Saihōji (the first character of its name denotes it as the "Western Temple") evoked for him the Western Mountain to which Master Liang, an ancient sage man whom he greatly revered, retired.

When Musō Soseki undertook the restoration of Saihōji, it already had a garden furnished with a pond. The monk enlarged the area of water, put in some islands, and, even though it was a monastery, built a dock for boating, just like ones the pleasure gardens from the Heian period had. But Musō undertook even more innovative changes. On one hand he built a path around the pond, so that one could walk around its circumference. In this way he inaugurated the genre of the promenading garden, which would become widespread from the seventeenth century on, as exemplified in the famous imperial villa of Katsura. On the other hand, breaking with the symmetry inherent in the *shinden-zukuri* style, Musō distributed the buildings in accordance with the terrain. On the west bank of the pond he built a multi-story reliquary pavilion, which was mirrored in the tranquil waters. This building was the prototype of the famous Golden and Silver Pavilions, which were built by the ostentatious Ashikaga shogun. Musō also had pavilions built for drinking tea—a beverage that Zen monks helped make popular in Japan—and also arranged for the construction of a "pavilion bridge," a kind of covered walkway that probably resembled the one that is still there today at Eihōji. As for the tea pavilions, these must have been Chinese-style kiosks. All these constructions were connected by galleries which, rather than being rectilinear as in the Heian period, wound around the features of the terrain like the Great Wall of China. This was all quite novel, even though the influence of the paradisal gardens of earlier times was still perceptible. But Musō also created at Saihōji a second garden.

*9 Rock garden at Saihōji Temple, Kyoto. By Musō Soseki, circa 1339.*

To the north of the pond a gate opens to the part known as Kōinzan. In going there one enters another world. After ascending a series of steep stone steps one discovers a garden that is quite different from the one below. In a dark wooded area an immobile avalanche of rocks seems to come down the mountain in a deafening silence (fig. 9). This garden consists simply in rocks which, over twenty meters or so, are grouped on three different levels. Of considerable size and similar in nature, most of these blocks have sharp edges. Not one of the rocks is standing upright, nor is in any way remarkable in itself. Those occupying the highest level are low, so as not to dominate the ensemble. All are positioned in such a way that the visual field seems to gradually become narrower from bottom to top, which produces an effect of depth. With exceptional rigor and perfect coherence, Musō accomplished the task of arranging a large number of rocks. This dynamic composition, which verges on the violent, offers a strange vision of nature, one in which a Zen monk tries to express his religious experience and project his personality onto the cold and silent world of stone.

The originality of this dry landscape garden is that is situated on a sloping site, in an open wood, and that it consists in rocks that come from the surrounding area. It appears natural: one sees such groups of rocks when on an outing in the forest. However—and this is exceptional in the art of Japanese gardens—the rocks used are in a sense recycled: they were previously used for a prehistoric necropolis nearby. But such is Musō's art that one hardly suspects that these rocks were worked on—unless in the case of two level rocks in the foreground, which look like steps on a staircase. Paradoxically, this composition looks much more natural than do those of most other dry landscape gardens, even though the latter contain no rock that has been fashioned or even touched up.

It might seem strange to use rocks from a sepulchre to construct a garden. But there is a passage in the *Laṅkāvatāra Sūtra,* a compilation of texts representative of Buddhist thought, which recommends ascetic practice under trees, in caves, and in funerary mounds. This is why Musō had no qualms about setting up a meditation place next to a field of tombs. Zen monks are in any case not liable to be frightened by profanation.

Some people see in this tableau of rocks a roaring waterfall or a raging torrent. In fact Musō wanted to evoke the Western Mountain where Master Liang spent so much time. The story is as follows: in twelfth-century China there lived a man by the name of Xiong. One day he was wandering in the forests of the Western Mountain when he came across a monk who appeared to be very old. Clad in a robe of woven leaves, and seated on a rock, he was meditating in the rain. Xiong remembered that centuries before a monk of high rank by the name of Liang had retired to this mountain. He went up to the old man and asked whether he was the venerable Liang. The only response the meditator gave was to point to the east. Xiong turned toward this direction, and was then about to question this strange old man further— but the man had disappeared. Xiong thought that he had been dreaming, but the spot where the ascetic had been sitting the moment before was completely dry, in spite of the rain.

The rock garden and the pavilion beside it formerly constituted Edoji, the "temple of the defiled world," by contrast with Saihōji, whose name evokes the Pure Land of the West. The former was a sacred place, closed to the public. Just the monks were allowed there, for the purposes of ascetic practice and meditation. Lay people were admitted only to the lower garden.

If the upper garden is more or less intact, the lower one

has, by contrast, changed its appearance in the course of the centuries—aside from the pond, which has retained its original contours. In particular, the soft carpet of moss, for which Saihōji is renowned these days, was not foreseen by Musō Soseki. This parasitical vegetation invaded the grounds only in the course of the Meiji era (1868–1912), at a time when the monastery did not have sufficient funds for the upkeep of the garden. In the fourteenth century the islands were carpeted with white sand. Along the borders of the pond the cherry trees would turn pink in the spring, and the maples would redden in the autumn. It was a radiant world, where one would come to walk and go boating while dreaming of the Paradise of Amida. But around a hundred meters away from this exquisite place, on the side of the mountain, a rough and arid site represents the world here below. The roughness of the angular rocks, which seem to tumble down the slope, cuts across the softness of the moss and the calm of the mirror of water, which no breeze ever comes to disturb.

In 1342 the shogun Ashikaga Takauji charged Musō Soseki with the task of transforming the villa of the retired emperor Go-Saga, which had been built a century earlier, into a Zen monastery. This is the origin of Tenryūji. When he arrived at Saihōji, Musō had found a religious site. Since there was already a Buddhist establishment there his task was relatively easy. But to make an imperial residence, which was designed for games and pleasures, into an austere Zen monastery was no simple matter. The residence was in the style of *shinden-zukuri:* to the south of the symmetrically arranged buildings was a pond with an island in the middle, which was connected to the bank by a small arched bridge. The pond had been used for boating and fishing. Musō undertook major works in order to refashion the pond: he shortened it and did away with the island and the culvert, but made up for this by furnishing it with numerous rocks. On the far side of the pond he constructed a "rock-fall" consisting of thirty or so rocks, which forms the center of the composition. To complement this he made three long, flat rocks, joined end to end, into the shape of a bridge. This bridge made of natural flagstones was the first of its kind in Japan. Near the culvert a group of pointed rocks suggests peaks forming a deep gorge. Several meters from the bank he placed other rocks, symbolizing Mount Sumeru. One of these, which juts out forcibly from the water, strongly resembles a rock that juts out of the pond at Mōtsuji, a monastery that was built in the twelfth century (fig. 11). This shows that the tradition of erect stones in the Heian period was still alive in the fourteenth century.

One of the distinctive features of Tenryūji is the relationship between the *hōjō* and the pond.[5] During the Heian period one went out in the garden for recreation. But here the pond is above all meant to be viewed from the building. It is not large enough for boating, and the stone culvert is decorative rather than functional. In short, the garden is not a place for amusement: it has become a site for contemplation. That such a change should take place between Saihōji and Tenryūji, within the space of just a few years and in two works by the same man, is an eloquent testament to the rich-

*10 Garden of Tenryūji Temple, Kyoto. By Musō Soseki, circa 1345.*

ness of Musō Soseki's imagination and his creative genius. It should also be noted that the pond is no longer situated to the south, according to tradition: it is on the west side of the residence, so that the nearby mountain forms the background. And to the left the mountain Arashiyama is incorporated in the garden, according to the technique of "borrowed landscape" (*shakkei*), for which the famous garden maker Kobori Enshū will become renowned in the seventeenth century. Here again Musō is an important precursor.

As far as pictorial expression is concerned, the garden of Tenryūji combines two styles: the pond nestled against a hill whose rounded mass is integrated into the space is in the traditional manner of *Yamato-e*. But the arrangement of the rocks is reminiscent of Song dynasty landscape painting. There is even a definite allusion in that the dry waterfall bears the name "Longmen," referring to the famous rapids of Longmen on the upper reaches of the Yellow River. Song landscape painting was not yet widely known in Japan at this time, so that we have to assume the influence of a Chinese monk who would have advised Musō about the art of the garden. When he lived in Kamakura, Musō had occasion to meet Zen masters who had come from the mainland.

A number of gardens have been attributed to Sesshū (1420–1506), one of the greatest Japanese painters in monochrome. The garden of Jōeiji in the city of Yamaguchi is the most remarkable of them, and also one whose authenticity is least contested, since the painter lived for a long time in this provincial town (fig. 12). Centered around a pond whose grassy banks are dotted with rocks, this gently undulating garden is set on a wooded hill that serves as a frame for it and extends it into the nature surrounding it. The fact that a water garden and a dry landscape garden are next to one another, without being interdependent, is reminiscent of Saihōji, and the organization of space is similar. Moreover, in the area that rises from the pond up to the back of the garden there is an arrangement of rocks evoking "the Longmen waterfall," which carp go up—symbolizing success—as at Tenryūji. Like Musō Soseki, Sesshū was a Zen monk. But he was also, and above all, a landscape painter. In search of picturesque sites, he traveled all over Japan and even went to

11 *Remains of the paradisal garden of Mōtsuji Temple, Hiraizumi, Iwate Prefecture. Twelfth century.*

China, where by his own account he learned a great deal from nature. This is why some of the rocks in the garden of Jōeiji bear the names of celebrated mountains, such as Lushan, hymned by the Chinese poets, and Mount Fuji, a sacred mountain par excellence. But aside from the symbolism, it is quite possible that in order to create this original garden the author was inspired by a site in the Yamaguchi area: the plateau of Akiyoshi-dai, whose uneven terrain is covered with grasses and strewn with blocks of limestone.

12 *Garden of Jōeiji Temple, Yamaguchi, Yamaguchi Prefecture. Attributed to Sesshū, second half of the fifteenth century.*

## The Garden of Ryōanji

During the fifties an American citizen by the name of Bean Porter, who described himself as a physician, writer, artist, and editor, praised the garden of the Ryōanji Temple in the following terms: "It is a beautiful poem, a simple statuary, a deep philosophy, a wonderful picture, a magnificent architecture, a lovely music, and a profound religion." This is no doubt extending the borders of the dithyramb a bit too far: the Zen garden requires a more sober approach. But what is this mysterious monument of stones (figs. 13–15)?

Name and address: Rock Garden, Ryōanji Temple, Kyoto, Japan
Date of birth: late fifteenth or early sixteenth century
Area: around 200 square meters
Contents: fifteen rocks, in five groups of two, three, or five
Special name: "garden of emptiness" (*mutei*)

This is the official information concerning this disconcerting garden.

The temple of Ryōanji was founded in 1450 by Hosokawa Katsumoto, a warrior and prime minister. But this founding was to prove ephemeral. In 1467 the famous Ōnin Civil Wars broke out, in which Katsumoto took an active part, and in the course of the ten years that it lasted the capital city was almost completely destroyed. Ryōanji by no means escaped the disaster, and was burned to the ground. The rebuilding of the temple was undertaken in 1488 by Hosokawa Masamoto, the son of Katsumoto. But it is unlikely that the present garden dates from that period, since the area to the south of the *hōjō*—where the garden is presently situated—was at that time reserved for certain ceremonies, which suggests that it was completely empty. Furthermore, the *hōjō* was not completed until 1499. The garden was probably created between that year and 1507, the year Masamoto died.

In 1797 Ryōanji fell prey to fire once again and underwent important transformations during its reconstruction. However, the rock garden does not seem to have suffered too much from these events. In fact, among old gardens it is the one whose former appearance remains best preserved. This is because it contains neither water nor plants, which are subject to change: trees die, springs dry up, ponds dry up and gradually accumulate humus and detritus. But when a garden is stripped of its vegetal covering and emptied of the element of water, the rocks are all that remain, and these, like the bones of a skeleton, defy time. Stone is immutable— at least on the human scale—and almost indestructible.

The terrain of the garden at Ryōanji is surrounded by a trough filled with pebbles, which ensures that rainwater runs off. To the west and the south the space is enclosed by a low wall topped with a tiled roof. To the east there is a white-washed wall, and to the north a wooden verandah that runs the length of the adjacent building. Behind the low wall there is a screen of red pines and maples, which cuts the garden off from the world outside. But it seems that the view originally stretched into the distance. And above the rocks and the gravel, the sky, like an immense canopy of changing colors, crowns the garden.

The terrain is furnished with only fifteen grayish rocks of various sizes, on a sheet of light gray gravel. They are arranged in five groups of two, three, or five. Adding a touch of dull green to the neutral colors of the tableau, moss surrounds the base of the rocks, like forests around the bases of high mountains.

Of all the dry landscape gardens from the Muromachi

period, the one at Ryōanji is the most concise. At Daisen-in, where the area is only half the size, there are more than a hundred rocks, which were chosen for their color, veining, or special shape. In their isolation, the fifteen rocks at Ryō-anji hardly offer much interest. They are, all in all, ordinary enough, and would probably not attract the interest of someone coming across them while walking in the depths of the forest, on a mountainside, or by the seashore. Only two of the rocks are erect, but they are not very tall; the others lie or rest on the ground. None of them imposes by virtue of any remarkable feature; they all mutually reinforce each other's value. In this way the equilibrium of the ensemble is flawless.

If the materials are simple, the composition is by contrast very complex, insofar as the garden combines several groups of rocks that together form a whole without losing any of the independence of their individual forms. The principle that governs the arrangement of the rocks consists in disposing the satellite elements not far from one or several central rocks, then introducing a third group of rocks known as "invited" rocks. At Ryōanji the principal and secondary groups are counterbalanced by three other groups that constitute an autonomous arrangement at the same time as they form a tertiary group.

The gardens created by Musō Soseki and Sesshū are fairly large in size and are situated in natural settings. The garden of Ryōanji is relatively small, and seems to be taking refuge behind its walls. One of its distinctive features is that the terrain is perfectly flat and rigorously geometrical, which

serves to reinforce its abstract character. To construct a garden on completely artificial ground was a novelty. This area bordered by walls is also a kind of three-dimensional painting.

The garden of Ryōanji not only eschews vegetation and water but also rejects all figurative shapes. One sometimes sees rocks in other Zen gardens arranged in such a way as to suggest a waterfall, a river, or an undulating landscape, or else the configurations suggest a bridge or a boat. By contrast with the gardens of Daisen-in and Taizō-in, the composition here is quite airy, with most of its area being dedicated to emptiness and the materials being restricted to an absolute minimum. This tableau consisting exclusively of rocks and gravel is stripped down in the extreme, and this very austerity is one of the grounds of the fascination that the garden of Ryōanji exerts on the viewer.

The abstract dimension of this composition is such that some commentators refuse to call it a garden, arguing from the fact that its creator deliberately excluded most of the elements that ordinarily constitute a garden. But in fact the garden of Ryōanji was not so austere in former times: the warlord Toyotomi Hideyoshi (1536–98) went to Ryōanji one day to view the blossoms of a huge weeping cherry tree. It thus seems that in the sixteenth century it was the flowering trees that made the temple famous. One has to wait until the seventeenth century to find mention of the rock garden, which was originally only a secondary element and was eclipsed for a long time by the cherry tree. Then, when the tree died, one became aware of the beauty of the rocks and began to value them.

*13 and 14  Garden of Ryōanji Temple, Kyoto. End of the fifteenth or beginning of the sixteenth century.*

*15 Garden of Ryōanji Temple, Kyoto. End of the fifteenth or beginning of the sixteenth century.*

How then does one read this abstract tableau (fig. 16)? When one approaches the garden from the left, the eye is drawn first of all to the group of five rocks, which is both the most important and the most conspicuous. Then one's view glides toward a group of two, one of the more modest groups. From there three rocks divert one's glance toward the right; one's gaze then rebounds from two others to end up on the final group, which consists of three rocks. But this is only one way of approaching the garden, since one can then sit on the middle of the verandah. From this viewpoint one discovers that the composition follows an elliptical orbit. Rather, one comprehends the lines of force that animate the five groups and connect them to each other. In this oblong area—as in the illuminated scrolls that flourished from the twelfth to the fourteenth century—one's reading has to begin from the right-hand side, since Sino-Japanese writing moves from right to left. The three groups at the back consist of seven rocks altogether. This number is the key to decoding the rhythm that animates the space. The seven leads to the five, which forms the major group. Then, like a text written in "boustrophedon," the line turns upon itself, ricochets off in the opposite direction, and ends up at the far right in the foreground, with the last three rocks.[6] Thus ends the visual tour of the garden.

In addition to this rhythm of forms there is a numerical one, which is based on the series 7-5-3 and sustains the entire composition. The Chinese and Japanese think of uneven numbers as propitious. According to ancient Chinese thought, the odd numbers—which were celebrated in other times and places by Virgil and then Verlaine—are *yang,* while the even are *yin.*[7] This is why odd is superior to even. On the numerical scale the 5 is accorded special significance: situated in the middle of the first nine numbers, it is a symbol of the center. Hence the theory of the five primordial elements: wood (east), fire (south), earth (center), metal (west), water (north). This originally Daoist schema gave rise to the cosmic diagram of a central mountain surrounded by four others situated at the cardinal points. Thus 5, as the pivotal number, marks the axis of the world around which the four directions are arrayed. In the sequence of odd numbers the 3 and the 7 are closest to the central 5, and this is what produces the numerical triad so beloved by the Japanese.[8]

One of the formulas that is applied in Zen gardens consists in the establishment of three groups of rocks of three, five, and seven, for a total of fifteen. The garden of Ryōanji offers a variation on this theme: the fifteen rocks are arranged from east to west—or from left to right— according to the following melodic pattern: 5, 2, 3, 2, 3. This variation, which is rare if not unique, attests to the original- ity of the garden's creator.

What can these fifteen rocks represent—set, as they appear to be, in sterile gravel? Several answers to this ques- tion have been proposed, which has long been asked. During the Edo period (1603–1867) the most fantastical answers were given. One interpreter was able to distinguish in the garden the silhouettes of the sixteen *arhat,* no matter that one rock is missing from the total.[9] The author had to suppress one of these saintly personages in favor of the preference for odd numbers. The explanation furnished by Dōgen Donei is delirious, even though he was a monk at Ryōanji. According to this visionary, the garden is meant to be an illustration of the legend of Liukun, a provincial governor who lived in China during the Han dynasty (206 BCE to 220 CE). This man fulfilled his duties so virtuously that all the tigers of the region, being subjugated, took their young on their backs and fled by crossing the river. The fifteen rocks of Ryōanji are thus said to represent a tigress helping its progeny across the water.

More reasonable, but perhaps somewhat misleading

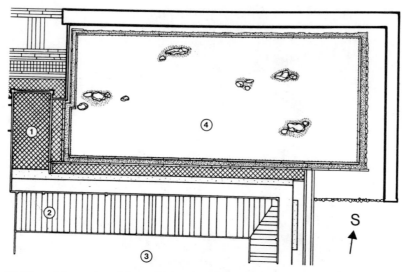

16 *Plan of the garden of Ryōanji Temple, Kyoto. End of the fifteenth or beginning of the sixteenth century.*

because overly simple, are the following interpretations: in many Zen gardens water is replaced by sand or gravel, which then suggests the sea or a river. So the rocks at Ryōanji could evoke the mountain-islands inhabited by the immortal hermits. This theme is often treated in Japanese gardens, and these legendary islands number three or five—and there are five groups of rocks at Ryōanji. Then again, this could represent a grand landscape, such as one would see from the window of a plane, as if the summits of high mountains were breaking through a sea of clouds. Or one could say that it is a case of the Five Sacred Mountains which, for the Chinese, symbolize the center of the world

*17* Linji in the process of
emitting a belch. *This
great master of the ninth
century was an expert in
eructation, which he held to
be one of the most efficacious
instruments of Zen
maieutics. Ink and light
colors on paper. Attributed
to Soga Jasoku, second half
of the fifteenth century.
Shinju-an, Daitokuji
Temple, Kyoto.*

and the four horizons, and correspond to the five primordial
elements.

The garden of Ryōanji has thus been interpreted in four
different ways. But why not raise the stakes? Could this sibyl-
line garden not simply be an eructation of rock, in the manner
of the great Chinese master Linji (Jpn., Rinzai), who would
belch in the faces of his pupils to help them on to the true Way
(fig. 17)? Or else could it not be a petrified stream of urine,

in the manner of Ikkyū, who pissed publicly on a Buddhist statue that he had been asked to consecrate (fig. 18)?[10]

But at the end of the day, are all these interpretive efforts—some more or less well founded, others completely off the mark—even necessary? The garden of Ryōanji is above all a work of art, and nothing will be able to explain its beauty or the fascination that it exerts, even though there is little that is a priori attractive about it. Perhaps it is preferable not to know the intention of its creator, nor the theme being treated. It is precisely because the significance of this garden remains vague that it is so rich in meaning: it is because it is shrouded in mystery that it offers everyone a large margin of fantasy.

Rather than interrogating in vain the fifteen rocks of Ryōanji, it is better, after a long contemplation, to lend an ear in order to catch their voices, which have been stifled by so many days and nights, and so much talk and noise. What are they saying, exactly? What silent words does this garden contain?

*18* Ikkyū Sōjun. *Colors on paper. Attributed to Bokusai, second half of the fifteenth century. National Museum of Tokyo.*

"I am nothing but blocks of stone on pieces of gravel. I am nothing but weight and silence, inertia and density. Nothing will ever learn my secret, or even whether I contain one. The only thing that can penetrate me is the strident cry of the cicada that pierces the heart of summer.[11] Be content to taste the raw beauty of my opaque flesh; look at me without saying a word and ask me nothing; be silent and try, through my hermetic body, to find yourself."

It is extremely difficult for most of us to admit that one can make a "garden" without trees and flowers, water or birds. How could the Japanese, who also love gardens with trees, flowers, and ponds, create a space as desolate and arid as the garden of Ryōanji? There is an expression in French whose pejorative character is significant: "It's a stone in my garden." Why did the Japanese have no compunction about distributing rocks in theirs?

As in other areas, the influence of China is far from negligible. In Chinese gardens the rocks are as important as are the beds of flowers in European gardens. This predilection for rock has its roots in the Chinese view of mountains, which since high antiquity were places impregnated by supernatural forces. Since religion and art were closely connected—formerly, at least—these beliefs acquired an aesthetic dimension, in such a way that rocks came to play a major role in the ornamentation of gardens. This tendency emerged during the Tang dynasty (618–907) and increased during the Song dynasty (960–1276).

The Chinese word for "landscape" is *shansui,* which

means "mountains and waters."[12] This term evokes the Islands of the Immortals, and also refers to the bipolar concept of *yang* and *yin*. To conjoin the rough hardness of rock with the soft fluidity of water produced great aesthetic pleasure. There was also an ancient belief—founded on a cosmogonic myth—according to which rivers are the blood that irrigates the body of the earth, while mountains are the bones. All this goes to explain the Chinese predilection for rocks.

To construct a garden using hardly any other materials than rocks presumes that these had a special significance in Japan—even if the idea of furnishing gardens with rocks originated in China. The cult of stone appeared in Japan as early as the Neolithic Era. The best evidence of this is the Ōyu stone circle (fig. 19), a kind of archetype of the arrangements of rocks in Japanese gardens. The composition is unique among the world's megalithic monuments: the vertical thrust of the central menhir contrasts with the horizontality of the lying rocks that radiate from this hub of an immobile wheel.

According to the ancient religion of Shinto, the gods manifest themselves in certain natural places or things, including mountains and rocks, which are therefore regarded as "divine bodies" (*shintai*). Mount Miwa is thus the object of a cult that, according to the archeologists, dates back to the Bronze Age. On this mountain is a "rock-seat" (*iwakura*)—a kind of sacred stone—similar to the rocks that ancient peoples venerated in numerous places in the Mediterranean Basin, of which one of the best-known examples is the stele that Jacob erected in Bethel after his famous dream. Like the sacred stone of the Bible, the *iwakura* is a point of contact between heaven and earth, a privileged place where humans can communicate with the gods. The "rock-seat" on Mount Miwa consists of a rock with several rocks of various sizes in front of it. Although this group is rough and probably natural, it is reminiscent of the rock arrangements in Japanese gardens. And even if there is no direct connection, it can be regarded as their spiritual ancestor.

Because Shinto is essentially a cult of forms and forces of nature, it is no surprise that the Japanese should experience such attraction for "true" rocks. Even when moved into a garden, the rock must not be retouched by human hands: it must stay intact, remaining in its pure state, for its purpose is to express the world just as it is, and its very essence. Patiently sculpted by waters and winds, it is the work of time, which operates slowly. The point is to respect the rough character of rock, since to work it is to desacralize it. In this connection, it is written in the Bible: "If you raise for me an altar of stone, you may not make it of sculpted stone, for in taking the chisel to the rock you will profane it" (*Exodus,* 20:25).

This profound respect for stone, based on a cult several thousand years old, partially explains the apparent simplicity of the garden of Ryōanji. Sober to the point of appearing almost banal, these fifteen rocks are very different from Chinese rocks, with their convoluted shapes and tortuous reliefs, riddled with holes like pockmarked skin, and so affected by erosion that one would think them artificial even

*19 Stone circle centered on a menhir. First or second millennium BCE. Ōyu, Akita Prefecture.*

though they are quite the opposite. It is true that Japanese gardeners were from time to time seduced by rocks of a singular character or with rare veining. But for the most part the materials they chose are discreet and unobtrusive. If the Chinese showed a predilection for playing with stones, the Japanese preferred to read on the faces of rocks a more serious and austere expression.

Even though their symbolism was of Buddhist or Daoist origin, the rocks adorning gardens were basically sacred objects according to the Shinto perspective. It is written in the *Sakuteiki* that one must observe certain rules in arranging the rocks, on pain of incurring a *tatari,* a term signifying a punishment inflicted by the Shinto gods on whomever should violate a taboo. For example, it was forbidden to set horizontally a rock that was initially standing up, or to set vertically a rock that was originally lying down. In this way, whether the arrangements were tinged by Buddhist thought or Daoist beliefs, the rocks in Japanese gardens retained the sacred character that had been conferred on them by Shinto; they remained suffused with the ancient indigenous religion. This means that in Japan the ground was especially propitious for the flourishing of Zen gardens.

Furthermore, the rocks at Ryōanji are placed on a graveled terrain situated to the south of the *hōjō*. This kind of space has its origins in Shinto: it is a case of a *niwa,* a term that nowadays means "garden," but formerly referred to the ritual space, covered with white sand or gravel, that was established in certain Shinto shrines. It was in this place that one received and celebrated the gods, offering them festivities and dances. A similar kind of sacred space—clean and pure—was situated to the south of the building where the emperor, who was also the country's religious leader, conducted the affairs of state.[13] One can see this kind of esplanade in the Imperial Palace in Kyoto, which was rebuilt in the nineteenth century in accordance with ancient plans: vast, covered with white sand, the only ornamentation it has is a mandarin orange and a cherry tree planted on the right and the left of the facade, respectively.

It thus appears that the garden of Ryōanji, constructed on level, bare terrain and situated immediately to the south of the *hōjō,* is an heir to the sacred spaces of Shinto. It was revolutionary to put a garden in the south court of a temple, since this area was traditionally reserved for the performance of rites. It is known that a ceremony was performed in this place in 1489, before the rocks were put in place. As a general rule, temple gardens were situated on other sides of the buildings, and especially to the east.

The rocks and the sacred areas of prehistoric times are thus the aesthetic source of the garden at Ryōanji. It is relevant in this context to note that the *Kojiki* mentions a certain Iwasuhime no Kami, the "Divine Princess Rock-Sand."[14] This divinity, who is considered to be an apotheosis of rocks and sand, could well be the symbol of the imprint of Shinto on the garden of Ryōanji.

## The Creators

One of the peculiarities of Zen gardens is that they are almost always anonymous, which further adds to their mystery. In spite of its renown, the garden of Ryōanji is no exception. While there is ample information about the construction of the garden of Saihōji, we know nothing about that of the garden of Ryōanji: there is no mention of it in any document from the period. It is not until the end of the seventeenth century that this rock garden begins to attract the attention of scholars. In 1682 a certain Kurokawa

20 *Garden of Ryōanji Temple, Kyoto. End of the fifteenth or beginning of the sixteenth century.*

reports that it was Hosokawa Katsumoto himself, the
founder of Ryōanji, who conceived of the garden of this
temple. In an another work from two years earlier, the same
Kurokawa says that the creator of the garden is Sōami (?
−1525), who was a painter and a decorator of interiors. A
third text, which is unsigned but dated 1689, attributes the
paternity of the garden to Katsumoto. But this claim is
hardly acceptable, since the original Ryōanji was reduced to
ashes during the Ōnin Civil Wars, in the course of which
Katsumoto died, in 1473. Even if one concedes that this
warrior designed the garden, if it had not been ravaged it
would at least have been damaged by fire.

As we saw earlier, the present garden of Ryōanji could
not have been created before 1499. One can thus imagine
that the creator, or at least the inspiring force behind it, was
Hosokawa Masamoto, the son and successor of Katsumoto.
This man was an eccentric, whose strange behavior astonished everyone. Perhaps it was he who had the idea for this
extraordinary garden. In any case, Sōami could have
designed the plans for it.

A son and grandson of painters under the patronage,
as he himself was, of the Ashikaga shogun, an artist in his
own right, and a Zen adept under the name Shinsō, this man
was no doubt capable of conceiving a temple garden. Since
the Heian period in Japan, the art of the garden had stood
in relation to pictorial art, and several famous painters
were also creators of gardens.[15] Moreover, the gardens of the
Muromachi period, as far as their plastic expression and the
thought underlying them is concerned, have special links

with the landscape painting of the Song dynasty. Now, Sōami was an accomplished landscape painter in the Chinese manner—even though there is admittedly no solid evidence of his also being a gardener. It is therefore prudent to renounce attributing the garden of Ryōanji to him.

Another figure who has been presumed to be the creator of this garden is Tessen Sōki, who was a monk at Ryōanji and a talented gardener. Moreover, he wrote a treatise on the art of the rock garden, in which he proclaimed his taste for simplicity of materials and abstract expression. But we know that Tessen retired to his native province of Mino in 1477, and so he had probably died by the time the garden was constructed.

If there is no documentation concerning the rock garden of Ryōanji from the fifteenth or sixteenth centuries, there is at least a precious, if tenuous, indication of its provenance. The second group from the east (the left) consists of a large block of granite and two small rocks of bluish hue, and there are two names inscribed on the back of the main rock. One is quite legible: Kotarō; the other has been half effaced by the elements and is more difficult to decipher: Hiko(?)-jirō. A text from 1491 makes mention of a certain Kotarō, as someone attached to a Buddhist temple, and this is probably the same individual. Again in 1491 this Kotarō went to gather moss for the garden of Shōsenken, at the Zen monastery of Shōkokuji. If the second "signatory" of the rock at Ryōanji is indeed Hikojirō, he would have been both a contemporary and a colleague of Kotarō. In 1490 Hikojirō participated in hydraulic work at the same garden of Shōsenken. And we know for certain that these men were *kawara-mono,* laborers from the lowest stratum of the social structure of that time.

If the various hypotheses put forward during the Edo period are not very satisfactory, these two signatures, one of which is clearly legible, constitute a document of incontestable authenticity. A skeptic could object that it is simply a case of graffiti engraved by visitors wanting to leave a trace of their visit at Ryōanji, but this is most unlikely, because the rocks in temples never carry this kind of scar. It is nonetheless surprising that these signatures should not be mentioned in the archives of Ryōanji: they are visible enough, and the monks who raked the gravel every day must certainly have been aware of them. But it is precisely because these are the names of mere laborers that the monks have kept silent about them: these names on the rock were a source of considerable embarrassment. It is, moreover, possible that some of the fantastic attributions that were made stemmed from a reluctance to reveal the truth.[16] Sōami, the famous painter, had to lend his name—no doubt without being aware he was doing so—to the work. The true creators of a garden that is now known worldwide are obscure, but not anonymous. Even though they were despised, and even humiliated, these two great artists were proud of their masterpiece, to the point that they inscribed their poor laborers' signatures on one of the rough rocks that make up this fascinating universe.[17]

But who were they, these laborers, and how were they able to gain entrance into the secret world of Zen gardens?

The first professional garden makers we know about in Japan were monks who were called *ishitate-sō* ("monks who arrange rocks"). Their existence is attested as far back as the eleventh century. Since the gardens of the Heian period were deeply informed by Buddhist thought, only monks were given the task of designing and constructing them. The greatest among them was Musō Soseki, the father of the Zen garden. He synthesized in his procedures all the gardening techniques that had been developed in the course of the Heian period, and was able to combine creativity with a synthetic spirit. Before him the majority of monks that made gardens belonged to the Shingon School, and being of infe-

*21 and 22 Garden of Ryōanji Temple, Kyoto. End of the fifteenth or beginning of the sixteenth century.*

rior rank they were in a sense lay brothers. Being a famous Zen monk, Musō was an exception, and this earned him the following criticism from a Shingon monk in 1344: "This incomparable Zen master Soseki, in spending his time planting flowers and trees, debased himself as a religious figure."

From the beginning of the fifteenth century laborers began to replace the monks as garden makers, and their entry into the scene was associated with the rise of Zen. At this time the shogun and warriors were attracted by this new sect and barely showed interest any longer in the older schools such as Shingon and Tendai. The traditional garden-making monks were thus somewhat superseded, even if their theories and procedures were not yet outdated. But the rise of Zen sounded the knell for these monks; their places soon became vacant and were taken by laborers.

Japanese society at that time consisted of several classes: aside from the nobility and the clergy there were, in order of precedence, the warriors, farmers, artisans, and merchants. Beyond this rigid social framework there were pariahs, whose origins are obscure. These "non-humans," as they were called, were also ranked hierarchically: the lowest stratum consisted of the *kawaramono,* a word that can be translated as "those at the edge of the water." These poor creatures were assigned the most sordid tasks: the execution of criminals, the slaughtering of cattle, and the stripping and tanning of skins. According to Buddhist ethics one may not kill even inferior creatures, and Shinto precepts forbid acts that go against cleanliness. The laborers were thus regarded as impure creatures, with whom one must avoid contact in order not to be polluted. The majority of them took refuge on the banks of the River Kamo, which runs through Kyoto from north to south. Their trades of killing, skinning, and tanning required large quantities of water, and this is one of the reasons they lived near the river. But the ground there was inhospitable because it was studded with stones, and, moreover, it was dangerous because of flash floods. In 1427 a flood destroyed more than a hundred shacks. The banks of the River Kamo were thus most insalubrious: during the great famine that claimed more than eighty thousand victims in the capital in 1461, people tried burying the dead in the dry riverbed. The laborers were forced to dig enormous communal graves capable of holding a thousand or even two thousand corpses. Then, when there was no more space for burying the corpses, they began piling up until they dammed the waters. The laborers, who lived on the riverbanks, had charnel houses under their noses and were forced to breathe the pestilence that emanated from them.

The pariahs were forced to carry out the most vile tasks, though certain among them did less repugnant work—even though it was still forced labor—since they were liable to fatigue duty. Masons and painters of buildings were recruited from this class, as were terrace diggers, well diggers, and garden makers.

This last activity is attested from as early as 1424, when we know that laborers were charged with marking, in the residences of the nobility and in monasteries, pines and plum trees worthy of being offered to the emperor for adorning his palace. It is thus reasonable to assume that these laborers were well acquainted with the gardens of the capital and that they were competent in arboriculture. At first, under the instructions of the monks, they had to dig ponds, make small hills, position rocks, and plant trees. In this way they were initiated into the art of the garden and became true experts who eventually supplanted their masters. It was primarily these men that built the Zen gardens of the Muromachi period, but because of their social position it was no doubt not easy for them to take on this role. One can imagine that

the art they developed gained in originality and depth precisely because of the difficulties it forced them to confront. From another perspective these men must have been powerfully motivated: it is true that, stuck as they were in this implacable medieval society in which they were almost imprisoned, they could never hope to attain any decent status; but in devoting themselves to less vile tasks than those which they were usually forced to perform, they could improve to some extent their image of despicable wretches.

Furthermore, the laborers suffered under yet another handicap: not being recognized as professionals—even though they were—they had no access to the treatises to which their masters committed their secrets. They had to acquire their knowledge bit by bit from the monks under whose rule they served their apprenticeship. And this was true up to the day when they superseded their masters. These laborers breathed new life into the art of the garden, which was becoming sclerotic through secular repetition, and, under the sign of Zen, they took the genre of the rock garden to its greatest heights.

It was probably in large part because the laborers were, socially speaking, marginalized as outcasts that they showed such originality. They were not afraid to transgress taboos and overturn traditional ways of doing things. One of them, for example, made a stream run not from north to south, as prescribed by the Daoist conception of space, but from west to east. And when he was reproached for doing so, he responded by saying that this direction symbolized the

23 *Garden of Ryōanji Temple, Kyoto. End of the fifteenth or beginning of the sixteenth century.*

progression of Buddhism from India to Japan. In taking such liberties the laborers innovated and revitalized the art of the garden.

But these artists almost all remained in the shade: heavy was the burden that weighed upon them. They were condemned to submit to their sad fate. A collection of documents on the art of the garden compiled in the fifteenth century mentions forty-five names of garden makers: the majority are monks, and most of the others are noblemen. Not a single laborer is mentioned, even though they were the true masters of the art at that time. Only one of these men received his due: Zen'ami (1386–1482), who was a protégé of the shogun Ashikaga Yoshimasa. A refined aesthete and enlightened patron, this shogun was able to put art before social prejudices, and there even developed some ties of affection between the young ruler and the old laborer. But this latter had to wait until the age of seventy-two before being recognized as a master of the art. If he had died before reaching this age, his name would never have been transmitted to posterity. This man—who was called "an artist without equal" and of whom it was said that he was "foremost under heaven . . . in the planting of trees and the placing of rocks"—opened the way for a new generation of garden makers and helped to improve the lot of his disenfranchised comrades. Nothing prevents us from supposing that the two laborers who built the rock garden of Ryōanji were among his disciples.

## Descendants and Divergences

All the Zen gardens that come after the one at Ryōanji are naturally a part of its legacy. The monks demanded original works, and the imagination of the garden makers was vivid, so that other currents developed, and different styles began to spread. Nevertheless, the fifteen rocks of the garden at Ryōanji weighed upon the destiny of the Japanese art of the garden.

Daitokuji is one of Kyoto's five great Zen temples.[18] A city within the city, this establishment is made up of about twenty areas each consisting of a subtemple furnished with a small garden. The most famous is Daisen-in, whose garden is regarded as the equal, or almost the equal, of Ryōanji. This garden unfolds from the north to the south around the residence of the abbot, the eastern part being the most important (fig. 24). Two large rocks standing next to one another suggest a waterfall descending from a high mountain and turning into a torrent. The impetuous flood flows through a gorge and passes under a bridge over an enclosed valley, broadens by eating into the rocky walls, and produces rapids that break through a dike. Then the landscape assumes another aspect: the torrent has become a river with a slow and majestic flow; it spreads out into a vast plain from which hills rise up (fig. 25). A boat unhurriedly follows the current of the pacified waters (fig. 26). Having run its course, the great river empties into an infinite ocean.

These magnificent landscapes, which also evoke the unfolding of a life, are situated on a terrain of only seventy

*24–26 The garden of Daisen-in, Daitokuji Temple, Kyoto. Circa 1513.*

square meters. This bespeaks the compactness of the garden and the prodigious talent of its creator.

Even though the ground is flat, the garden of Daisen-in gives a strong impression of relief. The space has a rare density, and there is not a single hiatus in the composition. The floor of the verandah around the building is quite low, so that it is only slightly above the level of the gravel of the garden. The horizontal rock next to the building is almost as

high as the verandah, thereby constituting a kind of link between outside and inside (fig. 27). The rock is so close that one can touch it from the verandah. Given its smallness, this enclosed space is almost like another room of the building, and this rock like a piece of furniture. It is said that the famous tea master Sen no Rikyū (1522–91) placed a flower arrangement on it when Toyotomi Hideyoshi came to visit Daisen-in. Standing in the northeast corner, the prinicipal rock is 2.2 meters tall, and the one next to it on the right is about 30 centimeters smaller. Both of them stand barely two meters from the verandah. The fact that the tallest rock is the closest to the building creates a perspective effect—with the second rock appearing more elongated than it actually is—and lends a depth to the garden. Sagaciously arranged starting from the principal rock, all the others consummately fulfill the function assigned to them. In this magnificent composition everything is calculated to the centimeter, so that in spite of the narrowness of the space and the number of rocks that occupy it, there is no impression of overcrowd-ing. A screen with a window divides the garden into two almost equal parts, and it is bordered by a walkway leading across the garden to the adjacent building. This is the abbot's private corridor. But the partition also plays a role in the composition of the garden: in dividing the space in this way, it offers more angles from which to look.

By contrast with the gardens of Saihōji and Ryōanji, the one at Daisen-in is not at all difficult to decipher: it is the transposition into three dimensions of a Chinese landscape painting from the Song dynasty. The pictorial character of

27 *The garden of Daisen-in, Daitokuji Temple, Kyoto. Circa 1513.*

this garden is further accentuated by the presence of several "figurative" rocks such as the ones that represent the bridge and the boat. Just as the landscape suggested by the garden at Ryōanji is abstract, the one at Daisen-in is given quite concrete expression.

One of the salient characteristics of the garden at Daisen-in is its smallness. It is true that the monks did not have at their disposal the space that rulers and noblemen had to build their gardens. But another factor came into play here: according to Zen thought, notions of "large" and "small" do not really exist. In his *Dream Dialogues* Musō Soseki wrote: "Originally there is no condition of large or small in any of the things of the universe: the large and the small are in the minds of human beings. They are nothing but illusory appearances that float in perverted hearts." And at the end of the fifteenth century the monk Tessen Sōki said: "The Five [Sacred] Mountains rise up like anthills, the deep ocean is envious of a frog's puddle. . . . No place is either far or near; a distance of 30,000 leagues shrinks to a foot and an inch." In short, the infinity of the universe can be condensed into a minute space. In the eyes of the Zen monk, the miniature landscape of Daisen-in has a spiritual dimension such that it reduces the park of Versailles to the size of a tiny garden. Pushed to the extreme, this vision of the world, this intentional conflation of the immense and the minuscule, issues in the arts of *bonseki* and *bonsai,* which originated around the same time as Zen gardens.[19]

Another feature of the garden of Daisen-in is the large number of rocks in it: there are about a hundred, by contrast with the fifteen at Ryōanji. Many of them were carefully selected on account of their evocative shapes or intrinsic beauty. Most of them have names, and are thus in a sense personalized, whereas the rocks at Ryōanji are cloaked in anonymity.

In stark contrast to the east garden with its abundance of rocks is the south garden, which has been left bare except for two hillocks of sand on the left side (fig. 28). Although situated in a Zen temple, this space has its source in Shinto. We recall that the "south garden" is a descendant of the

*28 and 29  The garden of Daisen-in, Daitokuji Temple, Kyoto. Circa 1513.*

sacred spaces of Shinto shrines and the ceremonial esplanades of imperial palaces. The conical piles of white gravel also have their origin in Shinto: they were kinds of reservoirs from which one drew in order to purify a space, and when a ceremony was conducted or a distinguished visitor received, a carpet of white gravel would be spread on the ground. The twin cones at the Kamigamo Shrine in Kyoto no doubt inspired the creator of the south garden at Daisen-in, where from a uniform surface only these two piles rise up like breasts of gravel (fig. 29).

The *hōjō* around which the gardens are arrayed was completed in 1513, so that the latter must have been constructed around the same time. According to the tradition maintained at Daisen-in, the creator was the painter Sōami, who painted the landscapes in the middle room of the building. But there is nothing to corroborate this claim. Sōami seems to have been considered a kind of patron to garden makers, simply because he was a talented landscape painter. Nevertheless, there is no garden that can be attributed to him with certainty. It is more likely that the monk Kogaku Sōkō, the founder of Daisen-in, was the one who conceived the embellishment of the terrain surrounding his residence. But the care with which the rocks were chosen and the art with which they were placed suggest that a true expert provided assistance. This was no doubt a laborer: an ancient inscription on a board in Daisen-in relates that a garden maker named Saburō proposed and commented upon a "planned area of sea and rocks" at the beginning of the sixteenth century.[20]

In the same vein is the garden of Taizō-in, one of the subtemples of Myōshinji (fig. 30). It is thought to have been designed by the painter Kanō Motonobu (1476–1559). In spite of its small size, the terrain is filled with rocks enhanced by shrubs that compose a magnificent landscape: in the middle of a lake of gravel there is an island connected to the hilly banks by two long bridges. Whether or not it is the work of a painter, this garden has an undeniably pictorial dimension. And its highly decorative character, which connects it with the miniature landscapes of Daisen-in, contrasts with the austerity of the gardens at Saihōji and Ryōanji.

On the other hand, the garden of Shōdenji Temple, which dates from the seventeenth century, is inscribed in the lineage of the garden of Ryōanji, of which it is a kind of transposition. Here vegetation has taken the place of rocks: azalea bushes clipped into round shapes are arrayed, as if foaming up from the ground of white gravel, in the pattern 7-5-3 (fig. 31). This bold idea is attributed to Kobori Enshū (1579–1647), Japan's most famous garden master. Another original feature of this garden is that far beyond the wall of lime-washed earth that encloses it there rises Mount Hiei, the highest of the hills surrounding Kyoto. This is a fine example of the technique of "borrowed landscape," which consists in integrating the distance into the restricted space of a garden in order to lend it an almost infinite depth. This procedure arose during the Muromachi period, but it was in Kobori Enshū's time that it attained full prevalence.

If laborers dominated the world of Zen gardens, they

30 *The garden of Taizō-in, Myōshinji Temple, Kyoto. First half of the sixteenth century.*

never eclipsed the monk Musō Soseki, whose work influenced the two Ashikaga dynasties that were the most enamored of culture and the arts. Dazzled by the garden of Saihōji, Yoshimitsu had the lustrous Golden Pavilion built, which was transformed into a Buddhist sanctuary after his death in 1408 (fig. 32). The large garden in front of the building still carries the imprint of the art of the Heian period, as revitalized by Musō: the pond is sprinkled with rocks and rocky islets furnished with miniature pine trees, which

*31 Garden of Shōdenji Temple, Kyoto. First half of the seventeenth century.*

symbolize cosmic mountains and mythical islands, exemplifying a quiet syncretism of Buddhism and Daoism.

The grandson of Yoshimitsu, Yoshimasa had more sober taste than his ancestor. The Silver Pavilion (fig. 33), which he built around 1482, is of more modest dimensions than the Golden Pavilion: the garden is also perceptibly smaller and less rich. Its appearance has changed considerably since the fifteenth century. Nowadays it is famous above all for its formations of sand.[21] But these latter were not

*33* (left) *and 34* (overleaf) *Garden of the Silver Pavilion, Jishōji Temple, Kyoto. Fifteenth to nineteenth centuries.*

made until the nineteenth century, to fill the void left by a building that was destroyed by fire. Nevertheless, the truncated cone reminiscent of Mount Fuji and the platform furrowed by small waves compose an arresting tableau (fig. 34). It is also a lunar landscape which, on moonlit nights, opens up the gates of reverie when the light from the blossoming sky cascades onto the sand and tints it silver. The large conical pile is surely a descendant of the immaculate piles that are set up in Shinto shrines. Since the Heian period

*32 Garden of Golden Pavilion, Rokuonji Temple, Kyoto.*

35  *Garden of the Katsura family, Hōfu, Yamaguchi Prefecture. First half of the eighteenth century.*

this symbol of purity that is sand assumed an aesthetic value. In the *Tale of Genji,* for example, there are celebrations here and there of the beauty of the white ground of gardens, which shines in the sun or glows in the moonlight.[22]

The garden of the Katsura family is located in the town of Hōfu, in Yamaguchi Prefecture, far from the capital (fig. 35).[23] It is unusual to find a work of such quality in the provinces. This one was apparently constructed at the beginning of the eighteenth century by Katsura Tadaharu, a samurai who was also a poet and practitioner of Zen. Bordering the residence on the south and east sides, the terrain forms a right angle. On a bed of white gravel, strangely shaped rocks are arrayed, among them the so-called "hare rock." According to an ancient Chinese belief, a fantastic tree—the *katsura*—grows on the moon, where a hare has its lair. Whence the allusive name. In fact it is a heavy rock that forms a slightly obtuse angle, and looks more like a seat than a hare.

Another garden in the line of descent from Ryōanji is the inner garden of Tōkai-an, in Myōshinji Temple, which dates from the nineteenth century (fig. 36). On a stretch of white gravel seven rocks of unequal size are laid out like gray rosary beads. The central one of the arrangement is the smallest—a bold decision. From this hub three rocks are arrayed on either side in two groups. The composition aligned along a rectilinear axis is symmetrical, making it almost unique among Japanese gardens.

Although it is five centuries old, the garden of Ryōanji continues to instruct to this day. The garden adjacent to the Gyokudō Museum, which was built where the painter Kawai Gyokudō (1873–1957) died, near Tokyo, is based on the same formal principles. Several large rocks from the nearby river, together with a long, low mass of azaleas, animate the space, which is enlarged by the landscape around it: the valley through which the Tamagawa River flows between wooded hills. This work,

36 *The inner garden of Tōkai-an, Myōshinji Temple, Kyoto. First half of the nineteenth century.*

37 *Garden of the Gyokudō Museum, Ōme, near Tokyo. By Nakajima Ken, 1960.*

which is a happy synthesis of tradition and modernity, was designed in 1960 by the landscape architect Nakajima Ken.

Every masterpiece is imperishable, at least for as long as human beings have the wisdom to respect and the intelligence to protect it. Every masterpiece is inexhaustible, like a vital spring whose life-giving waters continuously overflow. Such is the garden of Ryōanji, which was built in times of famine and civil war by laborers who were regarded as untouchables, built under the sign of Zen for the edification—or mystification—of the world.

This narrow waste of gravel, with several dwarf mountains with steep sides, never ceases to exercise its fascination upon posterity. In our century the number of visitors who cram into this space is most impressive, and loud is the hubbub that issues from the crowd, forming a screen between rocks and heart. But all one has to do is sit at the edge of the garden and stop up one's ears. Then the miracle happens. In the great silence that is thereby regained, the spontaneous beauty of these rough rocks surges forth, and their immortal chant ensues, the substance of which is this: Beyond the weight of matter there resides Spirit, without which one can never truly live.

# CHRONOLOGY

**Fourth century**    Formation of the Japanese empire, at the end of the Bronze Age.

**538**    Official introduction of Buddhism into Japan.

**612**    A Korean digs a pond in the garden of the palace of the Empress Suiko, and sets up a symbolic rock in it.

**Circa 620**    An island is built in the pond of the garden of Umako, the chief of a powerful clan of the Soga family.

**710**    The Empress Gemmei establishes herself at Heijō-kyō (Nara), which becomes Japan's first great capital.

**736**    The Chinese monk Daoxuan introduces Zen to Japan, without propagating it, however.

**794**    The emperor Kammu transfers the capital to Heian-kyō (Kyoto).

**804**    The monk Saichō goes to China, where he is initiated into Zen. The following year he returns to Japan and founds the Tendai School of Buddhism.

The monk Kūkai also reaches the mainland. On his return to Japan, in 806, he founds the Shingon School of esoteric Buddhism.

**Second half of the ninth century**   Activity of Kose no Kanaoka, a painter and garden maker.

**Late tenth to early eleventh century**   Activity of Kose no Hirotaka, a painter and garden maker.

**1052–53**   The prime minister Fujiwara no Yorimichi transforms his residence in Uji, near Kyoto, into a Buddhist monastery, Byōdō-in. The adjacent garden represents the paradise of Amida Buddha.

**Second half of the eleventh century**   Tachibana no Toshitsuna, son of Fujiwara no Yorimichi, edits the *Sakuteiki,* the oldest surviving treatise on the art of garden making in Japan.

**1141–59**   Fujiwara no Motohira rebuilds Mōtsuji Temple and endows it with a paradisal garden.

**1185**   Minamoto no Yoritomo seizes power and becomes the first samurai ruler (shogun). He establishes his capital at Kamakura, not far from present-day Tokyo.

**1191**   After spending four years in China, the monk Eisai transplants Zen to Japan.

**1294**   Musō Soseki enters the Zen monastery of Kenninji.

**1338**   Ashikaga Takauji founds the second dynasty of shogun. Kyoto becomes the capital again.

**1339**   Musō Soseki undertakes to restore the garden of Saihōji Temple.

**1342**   Musō Soseki begins remodeling the garden of Tenryūji Temple.

| | |
|---|---|
| 1397 | The shogun Ashikaga Yoshimitsu has the Golden Pavilion built. |
| 1424 | Laborers begin working as garden makers. |
| 1450 | The samurai Hosokawa Katsumoto founds Ryōanji Temple. |
| 1458 | The laborer–garden maker Zenami becomes the protégé of the shogun Ashikaga Yoshimasa. |
| 1467–1477 | The Ōnin Civil Wars ravage Kyoto. |
| 1482 | Ashikaga Yoshimasa has the Silver Pavilion built. |
| 1488 | Hosokawa Masamoto, son of Katsumoto, undertakes the rebuilding of Ryōanji, destroyed by fire in the Ōnin Civil Wars. |
| 1499 | Completion of the abbot of Ryōanji's residence. Probable beginning of the construction of the rock garden. |
| Second half of the fifteenth century | The painter-monk Sesshū builds the garden of Jōeiji Temple in Yamaguchi. |
| circa 1513 | Garden of Daisen-in, Daitokuji Temple. |
| First half of the sixteenth century | Garden of Taizō-in, Myōshinji Temple. |
| First half of the seventeenth century | Garden of Shōdenji Temple. |
| Circa 1655 | Completion of the garden of the Katsura Imperial Villa. |

| | |
|---|---|
| **Beginning of the eighteenth century** | Garden of the Katsura family at Hōfu. |
| **First half of the nineteenth century** | Inner garden of Tōkai-an, Myōshinji Temple. |
| **1960** | Garden of the Gyokudō Museum at Ōme. |

## The Role of Rock in the Japanese Dry Landscape Garden
*A Philosophical Essay by Graham Parkes*

Saihōji—recently better known as Kokedera, the "Moss Temple"—lies nestled against the hills bordering Kyoto on the west, and harbors the oldest surviving example of *karesan-sui*. When visiting the dry landscape there, the best strategy (after the obligatory calligraphy and chanting of the *Heart Sutra*) is to take up a position at the rear of the phalanx of visitors as it makes its way around the famous pond of the lower garden. This will allow one later to linger awhile in undisturbed contemplation of the upper garden, after the others have moved off down the hill to the main temple buildings and exit. From the steep path that leads up to the garden, one sees to the left a magnificent group of rocks floating on a bed of moss and arranged in the "turtle-island" style, evoking the Daoist Isles of the Immortals. This group was probably set originally on a sea of white gravel, which was dispersed and covered by moss during a period when the temple grounds were left derelict.[1] It is a wonderfully down-to-earth rendering of the paradisal Chinese *topos*. The angular shapes of the rocks together with their arrangement, which leaves spaces among them, make for a composition that looks perfect from whatever angle it is viewed.

The turtle-island group is like an overture to the main body of the work, the "dry cascade" (*karetaki*) in the uppermost part of the garden. Here fifty or so rocks in three tiers descend the hillside, evoking a waterfall deep in the mountains. Most of the rocks are covered with lichen and surrounded by "pools" of moss. They are bordered by some moderate-sized trees, several of which describe graceful arcs over the edges of the arrangement. The moss, together with the lichen that clothes the rocks in varying thicknesses, offers a remarkable array of colors: browns, dark grays, mauves, oranges, and many shades of sometimes iridescent green. A few miniature ferns and a scattering of dead pine needles add contrasting touches. The warm colors of the moss pools stand out against the cooler hues of the bare stone, and when wetted by rain all the colors become impressively more saturated. If the sun is shining, its rays filter through the trees and highlight different elements of the composition differentially. When the branches sway in the wind, light and shade play slowly over the entire scene, the movements accentuating at first the stillness of the rocks. Further contemplation brings to mind Zen master Dōgen's talk of "mountains flowing and water not flowing."[2]

In corresponding natural settings—what the Japanese call *shōtoku no sansui,* landscape "as in life"—adoption of the appropriate perspective can reveal rock configurations of remarkable beauty, in which all elements are in proper interrelation. The viewing area at the foot of the dry cascade is now quite restricted, allowing minimal variation of standpoint, but the composition is nonetheless breathtaking in its "rightness." Not even Cézanne, that consummate positioner of rocks in relation to trees—albeit in two dimensions— could have effected a more exquisite arrangement. Cézanne's work is invoked by the younger of the two female protagonists (both of whom are artists) in Kawabata's great novel *Beauty and Sadness.* The older woman, Otoko, has proposed a visit to Saihōji in the hope that she can "absorb a little of the strength [of this] oldest and most powerful of all rock gardens." But the experience turns out to be unexpectedly overwhelming. "The priest Musō's rock garden, weathered for centuries, had taken on such an antique patina that the rocks looked as if they had always been there. However, their stiff, angular forms left no doubt that it was a human composition, and Otoko had never felt its pressure as intensely as she did now. . . . 'Shall we go home?' she asked. 'The rocks are beginning to frighten me.'"[3] What is it about the power of this garden that makes it so disturbing that it verges on the frightening?

The hill behind the upper garden is named Kōinzan, after the mountain hermitage of the Tang dynasty Chan master Liang Zuozhu, and so some commentators claim that the tiers of rocks evoke the steep path leading up to his temple, and represent more generally the difficult ascent to the summit of Zen teaching and practice. Others see it as merely the remains of an actual series of steps leading to another building in the temple—as something crafted, but not really a work of art at all. Since the lower garden is known to represent the Pure Land (*jōdo*), the Western Paradise of Amida, and the upper garden the defilement of this world (*edo*), yet other scholars see the "turtle-island" group of rocks as evoking Mount Hōrai and the dry cascade as a way leading out of the world of defilement.[4]

Whatever the significance of this earliest example of the *karesansui* garden—and we shall be returning to it for a discussion of its unsettling atmosphere—several of its features point us back to China. And given the enormous influence of Chinese ideas and practices on the development of garden making in Japan, we do well to begin by reviewing that history.

## Rocks and Stone in China

Few civilizations have revered stone and rock as greatly as the Chinese (though the Japanese are foremost among those few). A cosmogonic myth from ancient China depicts the sky as a vast cave, and mountains as fragments that came loose from the vault of heaven and ended up on earth. These huge stone fragments in falling through the air became charged with vast amounts of cosmic energy, or *qi* (*ch'i*), before embedding themselves in the earth.[5] As in other places, there is prehistorical evidence in China of cults in which stone plays a key role. But China is distinguished by having records of rocks being arranged (in emperors' parks) dating back over two thousand years.[6] At first a prerogative of the imperial family, enthusiasm for stone and the mineral kingdom then spread to the literati, and it endures in the culture to this day.

By contrast with our sharp distinction between the animate and inanimate (with rocks falling on the lifeless side of the divide), the ancient Chinese world view understands all natural phenomena, including humans, as being animated by the psychophysical energy known as *qi*. This energy, with its polarities of *yin* and *yang,* ranges along a spectrum from rarified to condensed—forming a continuum, by contrast with our dichotomies between matter and spirit or physical and psychical. Rather than positing a world of reality behind and separate from the world of ordinary experience, Chinese thought has generally sought to understand the transformational processes that underlie the current world of appearances. Chinese medicine, acupuncture especially, is predicated on the idea of balancing *yin* and *yang* energies within the body, and harmonizing the flows of *qi* constituting the human frame with the larger cosmic circulation of energies outside it.

The two great powers in Chinese cosmology are those of heaven and earth, the prime manifestations of *yang* and *yin* energies. In this sense rock, as earth, is *yin;* but insofar as stone thrusts up from the earth in the form of volcanoes and mountains it is considered *yang.* In relation to the basic element of water, which is *yin,* rock in its hardness again manifests *yang* energy. The poles of *yang* and *yin* also connote "activity" and "structure," so that the patterns that emerge from the interaction between heaven and earth are understood as "expressions of organization operating on energy."[7]

John Hay's monograph *Kernels of Energy, Bones of Earth* takes its title from two texts cited in an entry on stone from an eighteenth-century encyclopedia.

The essential energy of earth forms rock.... Rocks are kernels of energy; the generation of rock from energy is like the body's arterial system producing nails and teeth....

The earth has the famous mountains as its support,... rocks are its bones.[8]

What is significant here is not so much the idea of rock as bone of the earth but of stone as a concentration of earth's "essential energy." Rocks are also called "roots of the clouds," an expression deriving from the mists that surround the collision of water with rock, and from the vapors that gather around the peaks of mountains or enshroud the tops of cliffs and ridges. Some of the rocks most admired by the Chinese resemble clouds, and in landscape painting mountains are often depicted not so much accompanied by clouds as themselves looking like heaps of cumulus.[9]

The science that deals with our relations to terrain and environment is called *fengshui,* usually translated as "geomancy" (earth divination), though the literal meaning is "wind water." The aim of *fengshui* practice is to ensure that the places in which one lives and works, from residences and gardens to offices and workshops, are set up in such a way that one's activities are harmonized with the greater patternings of *qi* that inform the environs. François Jullien writes eloquently of the "lifelines" (*shi*) that geomancy detects in the configuration of terrain. Drawing on a classic text by Guo Pu from the fourth-century, he writes: "Let us experience 'physics' as the single 'breath at the origin of things, forever circulating,' which flows through the whole of space, endlessly engendering all existing things, 'deploying itself continuously in the great process of the coming-to-be and transformation of the world' and 'filling every individual species through and through.'" This "vital breath" is itself invisible, though discernible in the contours of landscape. Not all places are alike: they differ according to the patterns and concentrations of the energy flowing through them. Since this *qi* is also what animates human beings, people living in sites where the circulations of the vital breath are more intense will flourish more energetically: "By rooting one's dwelling here rather than elsewhere, one locks into the very vitality of the world [and] taps the energy of things more directly."[10]

Since rocks of unusual size or shape are special conduits or reservoirs for *qi,* beneficial effects will flow from being in their presence. The garden thereby becomes a site not only for aesthetic contemplation but also for self-cultivation, since the *qi* of the rocks will be enhanced by the flows of energy among the other natural components there. In a work called

*Eulogy to the Lodestone,* Guo Pu wonders at the inscrutable operations and interactions of the phenomena that *fengshui* tries to fathom:

Lodestone draws in iron, Amber picks up mustard seeds.
Energy invisibly passes. Cosmic numerology mysteriously matches.
Things respond to each other, In ways beyond our knowing.[11]

Chinese thought is especially fond of analogies between microcosm and macrocosm, so that the sense of correspondence between rocks and mountains runs deeper than mere symbolization.[12] Mountains as the most majestic expressions of natural forces were regarded as especially numinous beings: Five Sacred Peaks stood for the center of the world and its four cardinal points. Rocks were thought to partake of the powers of the mountain less through their resembling its outward appearance than for their being true microcosms, animated by the same telluric energies that form the heights and peaks. The identity between rocks and mountains is emphasized in numerous treatises on Chinese landscape painting, or *shanshui* (literally: "mountains waters"). The introduction to the famous twelfth-century treatise by Du Wan, the *Yunlin Shipu* (Cloud Forest catalogue of rocks), begins: "The purest energy of the heaven-earth world coalesces into rock. It emerges, bearing the soil. Its formations are wonderful and fantastic. . . . Within the size of a fist can be assembled the beauty of a thousand cliffs."[13] This idea that the beauty of the macrocosm is concentrated in the microcosm will become a major principle in the art of the rock garden in Japan.

Given the traditional reverence in China for natural phenomena, it is not surprising that Buddhist thought should take a distinctively Chinese turn after being transplanted from India during the first century CE. The legendary patriarch of the Chan (Zen) School of Buddhism, the Indian monk Bodhidharma, by some accounts spent nine years after coming to China meditating in front of the rock face of a cliff. (Buddhist arhats are often depicted seated on pedestals of rock or in caves, and there is a famous painting of Bodhidharma in a cave of rock by the Japanese painter Sesshū.) A significant development took place in the early Tang dynasty (618–907), in which the Mahayana Buddhist extension of the promise of salvation to "all sentient beings," based on the "dependent co-arising" of all things, was taken to its logical conclusion. A philosopher by the name of Jizang wrote of the "Attainment of Buddhahood by Plants and Trees," and a later thinker, Zhanran from the Tiantai School, argued that "even non-sentient beings have Buddha-nature."[14]

Therefore we may know that the single mind of a single particle of dust comprises the mind-nature of all sentient beings and Buddhas. . . . Therefore, when we speak of all things, why should exception be made in the case of a tiny particle of dust? Why should the substance of "suchness" pertain exclusively to "us" and not to "others"? . . .

Who, then is "animate" and who "inanimate"? Within the Assembly of the Lotus, all are present without division. In the case of grass, trees, and the soil, what difference is there between the four kinds of atoms? Whether they merely lift their feet or energetically traverse the long path, they will all reach [Nirvana].[15]

The Tiantai School was transmitted to Japan (as Tendai Buddhism) by the monk Saichō, who picked up the line of thinking developed by Zhanran and was the first in Japan to write of "the Buddha-nature of trees and rocks" (*mokuseki bussho*). The seeds of these ideas would find especially fertile ground in the minds of some formidable Japanese thinkers during the following few centuries.

## Chinese Petromania and Litholatry

A central feature of ancient Daoist lore was the belief that a race of Immortals inhabited floating islands far in the eastern seas. This occasioned repeated attempts during the Qin and Han dynasties (from the third century BCE to the third CE) to discover these sites and find the elixir of immortality. As mentioned in the main text, rather than going out to search for their islands himself, the Han dynasty emperor Wudi (140–89 BCE) attempted to entice the Immortals by constructing rocky islands of his own in ponds of the palace garden. Since the floating Isles of the Immortals were mountains, they were inherently unstable, so the Lord of Heaven had instructed giant turtles to carry them on their backs to stabilize them. For this reason they are often represented in Chinese gardens as resting on turtle-shaped rocks rather than floating on the sea. Buddhist mythology too was influential on garden making: the notion of a huge mountain, Mount Sumeru, at the center of the universe and surrounded by mountains separated by oceans, as well as the idea of Amida's Western Paradise to which true believers would be transported after death, were easily assimilated to the Daoist view of the Isles of the Immortals. Representations of Amida's Paradise would later become common in Japanese gardens, as would "Shumisen" rocks standing for Mount Sumeru.

A rich merchant during the Han dynasty is remembered for having built an enormous garden renowned for the excellence of its rocks, and whose salient feature was an artificial mountain (*jiashan*) over thirty meters high.[16] This hubris—since in China only emperors and princes were supposed to display their wealth by building parks and gardens—brought dire results: the man was found guilty of "a crime" and executed. Nevertheless, the establishment of private estates gradually became customary, and the merchant's rock mountain established a tradition in garden making. During the reign of the Wei emperor Xiao Mingdi (early sixth century), a minister of agriculture created an estate known as "Mountain of Bright Beauty": "He built up a mountain as if it were a work of Nature, with piled-up peaks and multiple ranges rising in steep succession, with deep ravines and caverns and gullies tortuously linked."[17]

In the year 607 the Sui emperor Yangdi built a magnificent park near his capital of Luoyang. He had four enormous lakes dug, and several rocky islands built in each. Although this had been done before, the scale of his project was unprecedented, and Yangdi's "Western Park" is significant because of its influence on imperial gardens in Japan. The first official embassy from Japan arrived in Luoyang in the autumn of 607, and the visitors from the Eastern Islands were in all likelihood shown the Western Park. The earliest mention of a landscaped garden with a lake, adjacent to the Japanese imperial palace, dates from the year 611.[18]

The emperor Ming Huang, who ruled China for the first half of the eighth century, was famous for building a garden, located at a hot springs, which contained a lake with a miniature mountain of lapis lazuli in the middle. This style also endured, for when Kubilai Khan (grandson of Ghengis) moved his capital to Beijing several centuries later, he had gardens built and parks furnished with lapis lazuli. Marco Polo appears to have been suitably impressed: "The rock is intensely green, so that trees and rocks alike are as green as green can be, and there is no other color to be seen."[19] It is sad that such monochrome extravaganzas can now be seen only in the imagination.

Shortly before the Japanese Tendai founder Saichō was born, in the year 753, the eminent Buddhist monk Jianzhen (Jpn., Ganjin) finally succeeded, after several abortive sea voyages, in making his way to Japan. He took with him many cultural items from the Tang, especially Buddhist scriptures and works of art, and he was soon invited by the emperor Seimu to establish a Buddhist temple in the capital of Heijō-kyō (the present-day Nara). Among the artisans that accompanied him were said to be garden makers, who will have found the Japanese soil well prepared for their art. The timing was auspicious, since the practice of making rock gardens attained a special degree of flourishing during the Tang dynasty.

The scholar-poet and high official Li Deyu built a famous rock garden in his estate near Luoyang, in which he arranged spectacular specimens brought in from many different parts of the country. The most spectacular came from Lake Tai (Tai Hu, also known as "Grand Lake") near Suzhou and Shanghai, in the heart of literati culture in the southeast. Li dignified the best rocks in his collection by having the words *youdao* ("possessing the Way") incised on them, and such inscriptions became common practice for enthusiasts.[20] The other great rock connoisseur of the period was his rival Niu Sengru, who also built a celebrated garden near Luoyang. The poet Bai Juyi was a friend of both men, and he produced a number of poems celebrating the beauty of their rock collections. The earliest description we have of a Taihu rock, which was to become the most highly prized kind in China, comes from one of Bai's poems.

Its controlling spirit overpowers the bamboo and trees,
Its manifested energy dominates the pavilions and terrace.
From its interior rise quiet whispers,
Is it the womb of winds?
Sharp swords show in its angular edges,
Their ringing resonance clearer than jasper chimes.
Its great shape seems to move,
Its massive forces seem on the brink of collapse.[21]

The geology of the Lake Tai area is remarkable in that the rock there is formed from limestone deposits nearly 300 million years old.[22] These ancient formations were corroded into extravagant shapes when the area was covered by sea, and were then worked and sculpted by the action of hard pebbles in the lake during storms. Especially fine specimens of these Taihu rocks—which look like frozen billows of ocean spume, or enormous stone fungi burgeoning into the air, or extravagant coral formations poised in an invisible ocean—would often stand alone as the centerpieces of famous gardens. After being touched up by human hands, they would sometimes be submerged in the lake again until they re-acquired the appropriate patina.

A more prosaic description of Taihu rocks is to be found in Du Wan's *Cloud Forest Catalogue:* "They are hard and glossy, with strange configurations of hollow 'eyes' and twisting peaks. . . . They have a net of raised patterns all over, their surfaces covered with small cavities, worn by the action of the wind and waves. These are called '[crossbow] pellet nests.' When these stones are tapped, they resound slightly. . . . [The smaller ones] may be used in building artificial mountains which, when set among spacious groves, are a magnificent sight."[23] This passage articulates several criteria for fine rocks, some of them distinctively Chinese. Eventually three primary desiderata were codified in the course of the Qing dynasty: *shou* ("leanness"), *zhou* ("surface texture"), and *tou* ("foraminate structure" characterized by multiple holes and openings).[24] The "lean" means that the rock should be without any kind of "fat" or excrescences that would obscure the expression of its internal structure or energy. The surface texture was similarly valued as an indication of the forces that had formed the rock. Foraminate structure was prized for being expressive of the transformations that make up the world as a whole and the interplay of void and form. This last desideratum was not among the features deemed important by connoisseurs in Japan (since nothing like the Taihu type of stone is to be found there).

The Chinese tradition tends to revere nature as "the greatest of all artists," in consonance with the Daoist ideal of *wuwei*: nondisruptive action in harmony with natural transformations. The great artist engages in *dou zaohua,* "plundering [the natural processes of] making and transforming," and takes these creative processes "as his master and teacher."[25] But the Chinese art of the garden does not shrink from perfecting natural products when necessary: from the evidence in the *Cloud Forest Catalogue* Edward Schafer concludes that "twelfth-century connoisseurs seem not to have put a premium on 'natural' stones."[26]

The seventeenth-century garden manual by Ji Cheng, the *Yuanye* (Craft of gardens), offers definite encouragement to improve on nature's work. Simply to move rocks to a garden is already to "denature" them in a sense, but the arrangements are meant to enhance their natural vitality: "Rocks are not like plants or trees: once gathered, they gain a new lease of life." Stone always has to be cleaned after being excavated, but certain kinds of rocks "may have to be shaped and carved with adze and chisel to bring out their beauty."[27] Such exhortations to apply the craftsman's tools are rare in the Japanese literature. The *Yuanye* advises that the rocks used for the peaks of artificial mountains should be larger at the top than below, and fitted together so that "they will have the appearance of being about to soar into the air."[28] Sometimes the effect of these artificial mountains is comparable to that of the Gothic cathedral, where the aim is to counteract the weight of the stone and lend it lightness. Rocks in Japanese gardens by contrast generally advertise rather than conceal their weight, though their placement is often designed to exhibit their vitality in the way they thrust up from beneath the ground.

The best Chinese rock will sound as well as look impressive: when tapped, it should give forth "a clear tone" (reminiscent of the stone chimes used in Chinese court music). A prime example is the sonorous Lingbi rock, which comes from a place called "Stone Chime Mountain." According to the *Cloud Forest Catalogue:* "When still in the soil, these rocks grow in various shapes according to their size. Some form animals, others mountain ranges with cliffs pierced by cavities. . . . Some shapes are more blockish, while others are flattish, [with patterns] forming clouds, sun and moonlight, and Buddhist images, even scenery of the four seasons."[29] The first distinction is generally applicable, between the "mountain" type of rock (including a kind known as "stone bamboo shoots") and the "zoomorphic" type (including Taihu rocks). The latter never became as popular in Japan, being domestically rare, nor was the sound emitted when tapped a major desideratum.

During the Song dynasty, an era distinguished by its peerless landscape painting, some connoisseurs of rocks valued them even more highly than paintings. The eleventh-century scholar-official Su Shi offered a hundred pieces of gold for a miniature rock representing a well-known mountain in Anhui, and famously claimed that the "Chouchi rocks" in his collection were worth as much as works by the master of Tang dynasty horse painting.[30] Like many scholar-officials Su was also a poet (under the name Su Dongpo), and a poem he wrote during a sojourn in the beautiful landscape around the sacred mountain of Lushan will later play a key role in Zen master Dōgen's exposition of his philosophy of nature.

Su Shi's contemporary, the poet Mi Fu, has been proposed as "the ultimate connoisseur of rocks in all of China's history." On taking up an appointment as a magistrate in the Wuwei District, which was renowned for the quality of its stone, he noticed a magnificent rock in a garden of the official precincts. Overwhelmed with admiration, he immediately made obeisance to it, and from then on addressed it respectfully as *Shixiong* ("Elder Brother Rock"). The episode became a favorite theme of painters, who delighted in assimilating the poet's shape and attire to the contours and patterns of the much larger rock.[31] The frequent depictions in painting of the isomorphism between human and stone attest to their enduring affinity in the Chinese tradition.

Mi Fu was also a painter, and his work resembled the "stone screens" that have long been a common item of Chinese furniture. The veining of the marble used for these screens exhibits "traces of mineral combinations of pure limestone and sedimentary layers of clay mixed with organic material or iron oxides which the limestone has recrystal-lized," which produce by way of "natural painting" patterns that look like landscapes.[32] Also known as "dreamstones" or "journeying stones," they have always been avidly collected by scholars and officials for the decoration of their residences, and several different kinds are described in Du Wan's catalogue.

As northern Song landscape painting began to flourish in the course of the tenth century, resemblance to depicted mountains became a feature that connoisseurs looked for in rocks. A traditional condition for successful landscape painting in China is *qi yun sheng tong,* which refers to the artist's ability to let his work be animated by the same *qi* that produces the natural phenomena he is painting. So rather than attempting to reproduce the visual appearance of the natural world, the artist lets the brushstrokes flow from the common source that produces both natural phenomena and his own activity. This condition was easily adapted to the art of garden making, where the very elements of the artist's craft are natural beings, which are then artfully selected and arranged in order to reproduce harmonies in the natural world outside the garden within a subtly organized setting.[33] When Song landscape painting reached Japan, it exerted a similarly inspiring influence on garden makers there, especially in their selection and arrangement of rocks.

The emperor that ruled China for the first quarter of the twelfth century, Huizong, was an accomplished painter as well as a connoisseur of gardens. Possessed by a passion for rocks that amounted to obsession, he built a huge park to the northeast of the capital at Kaifeng in which he constructed several artificial mountains. In one garden an enormous mountain of rocks, with "ten thousand layered peaks" was said to have risen to a height of seventy-five meters. The emperor had a special love of strangely shaped stone (including Taihu, naturally) and filled his park with the finest zoomorphic and anthropomorphic specimens he could find. According to a contemporary account: "They were all in various strange shapes, like tusks, horns, mouths, noses, heads, tails, and claws. They seemed to be angry and protesting against each other."[34] What fascinates about such stone is the way natural processes sculpt the apparently most inert of the elements into the shapes of more complex forms of animation such as plants and animals.

At the western entrance to the park Huizong placed a rock some fifteen meters high. "Other rocks on the side had various forms. Some looked like ministers having audience with the Emperor. They were solemn, serious, trembling and full of awe. Some were charging forward as if they had some important advice or argument to present."[35] The Confucian tradition is vitally embodied in these principles of arranging rocks in such a way that elemental presences are mimetic of social relationships. (The Japanese will later borrow some of their names for groups of rocks from Confucian social configurations.) Huizong gave names to the most spectacularly anthropomorphic rocks, which he had inscribed on them in gold. Although the park was called *Genyue,* "Impregnable Mountain" or "Mountain of Longevity," the emperor expended so much of his fortune on it that the extravagance eventually cost him the empire—and all his gardens and mountains with it.

Rock never lost its importance in Chinese culture, being eventually incorporated into the novelistic imagination as well. One of China's best known novels, the seventeenth-century *Dream of Red Mansions* by Cao Xueqin, was originally entitled *The Story of the Stone.* The hero Jia Baoyu (*baoyu* means "jade treasure") begins life as a rock—albeit a talking rock—is transformed into a human being, and later becomes a rock again, who then recounts "the story of the stone."

If lithomania never reaches the heights in Japan that it attained in China, it nonetheless runs deep, and we shall see many—though not all—of the grounds for enthusiasm over stone prove fertile in the Eastern Islands. Emblematic is a passion for a particular rock—a passion that was shared by two of the greatest figures in modern Japanese history. The warlord Oda Nobunaga was, in his nonviolent mode, a connoisseur of gardens. As such he eventually acquired the most famous stone specimen in the country, the "Fujito Rock," and when he had a garden made for the last Ashikaga shogun at one of his palaces in Kyoto, he transferred this rock from his own garden with unprecedented pomp. "Nobunaga had the rock wrapped in silk, decorated with flowers, and brought it to the garden with the music of flute and drums and the chanting of the laborers."[36] Toyotomi Hideyoshi, an army commander, later purchased it for the unprecedented sum of "a thousand *koku* of rice." When

Hideyoshi seized power after Nobunaga was killed in 1582 he immediately had the Fujito Rock transported to his new palace, and at the end of his life he installed it in a place of honor in a special garden he built at Sambō-in. This rock was one of the most valuable items in Hideyoshi's not insubstantial estate after he died.

## Japanese Treatises on Garden Making

At first sight the dry cascade at Saihōji gives the impression of being situated in a sacred grove, a place of natural numinosity. The tensions set up by the soaring arcs of the surrounding trees and the angular density of the rock arrangement, between the stillness of the stone and the dynamism of the descending-tiers composition, imbue the site with an almost supernatural power. Anyone acquainted with the indigenous Japanese religion of Shinto is going to feel the presence here of *kami* in high concentrations. As mentioned in the main text, Shinto shares with many other religions a view for which the entire natural world is animated and pervaded by spirits. Rocks in particular were thought to be inhabited by various *kami,* or divinities, and the more impressive ones (*iwakura*) were treated with special reverence as abodes of divine spirits. It was a natural step to then supplement nature by building piles of rocks in order to attract *kami* to a particular place, and these became the prototypes of the arrangements that would grace Japanese gardens in later centuries. Since rocks were regarded as numinous long before the importation of *fengshui* and garden lore from China, their role in the Japanese garden became ever more important.

The upper garden at Saihōji manifests several antinomies. Although the scene looks natural at first sight, the composition instantiates a highly sophisticated design. Whereas the rocks themselves appear natural, albeit selected for their mainly horizontal shapes, they are in fact hewn (as components of a former burial mound). And as a dry cascade the composition presents, and makes strangely present, water that is literally absent. Several of the larger rocks have vertical streaks and striations, like the "waterfall rocks" (*taki-ishi*) often found in Japanese gardens, where the streaks create the illusion of a cascade. Some water does, of course, run down these rocks in heavy rain, but the mossy ground surrounding absorbs the runoff, so that no actual streams develop to spoil the effect of a cascade that is dry in all seasons.

François Berthier has mentioned what is perhaps the most powerful effect of this garden: if one can arrange to contemplate it alone, on a windless day the almost total silence is occasionally interrupted by the deafening roar of a waterfall that is not there. One is again reminded of Dōgen: "When the voices of the valley are heard, waves break back upon themselves and surf crashes high into the sky."[37] It is perhaps the evocation of an absence through two sensory dimensions at once that accounts for the dry cascade's strange power. The arrangement of the rocks induces the viewer to see a cataract that isn't there, and the imaginative projection of downflowing water seems to animate the motionless rocks with an unsettling movement. The effect is enhanced by the auditory hallucination of rushing waters—a disturbing experience for visitors unaccustomed to hearing things that aren't there. But it's reassuring to know that hearing with the eyes is not regarded as abnormal by Zen masters: in discussing the mystery of how nonsentient beings preach the Buddhist teachings, Dōgen quotes from a poem by the Zen master Tōzan Ryōkai who says, "If we hear the sound through the eyes, we are able to know it."[38] (More on this in the last section.)

The gardens at Saihōji are attributed to the Zen monk Musō Soseki (1275–1351), who lived some three generations after Dōgen. (The *seki* in his name is, appropriately, a reading of the graph for "rock.") Musō wrote a poem with the title *Ode to the Dry Landscape* (*Kasenzui no in*), which begins:

Without a speck of dust's being raised,
the mountains tower up;
without a single drop's falling,
the streams plunge into the valley.[39]

Simply by arranging rocks in the upper garden of Saihōji, the author transforms a hillside into the face of a mountain, and with not a drop of water in sight, cataracts rush loudly down.

Scholarly opinion is divided on the question of Musō Soseki's authorship of the gardens at Saihōji and Tenryūji, and since he was already in his sixties when he came to Saihōji in 1339, he may well not have had much of a hand in the actual building of the garden.[40] But given that he had been working in the field for the previous three decades, it is likely that he contributed much to the design of the gardens at both temples. In any case he wrote eloquently about landscape, and what he says helps us understand the aesthetic effect of the two remarkable gardens whose designs are attributed to him.

Musō was an energetic and charismatic teacher who not only gained a large popular following but also won considerable influence with those in political power. This naturally turned some resentful types against him, and they branded his work with gardens as frivolous and his love of nature as indicating attachment to worldly pleasures. There is a passage in his best-known work, the *Muchū mondō* (Dream dialogues), in which he responds by distinguishing between various attitudes toward landscape and gardens and invoking the example of the poet Bai Juyi (part of whose poem in praise of Taihu rocks is cited above).

Bai Juyi dug out a little pond, planted bamboo at its edge, and loved this above all else. The bamboo is my best friend, he would say, because its heart is empty, and because the water is pure it is my master. People who love a fine landscape from the bottom of their hearts possess a heart like his. . . . Those who experience mountains, rivers, the great earth, grasses, trees, and rocks as the self's original part [*jiko no hombun*], though they may seem by their love of nature to cling to worldly feelings, it is precisely through this that they show themselves to be mindful of the Way [*dōshin*], and they take the phenomena that transform themselves into the four elements as topics of their practice. And when they do this aright, they exemplify perfectly how true followers of the Way love landscape.[41]

Those who surround themselves with a small landscape in the form of a garden gain nourishment from nature because its self-transforming elements are "the self's original part," out of which "all things arise." Through advocating the benefits of communion with the natural world in this way, against criticism from narrower souls, Musō contributed to the increasing valorization of nature in Zen thinking and practice.

The dry cascade at Saihōji is the most famous ancestor of the Zen gardens in the *karesansui* style, even though dry land-scapes date back to the Heian period. The earliest surviving manual for garden design is the *Sakuteiki* (Notes on garden making), attributed to the eleventh-century nobleman Tachibana no Toshitsuna. Even though the text deals with the Heian period pleasure gardens of the nobility with their ponds and streams, a section near the beginning contains the first mention of *karesansui* in the literature. "Sometimes rocks are placed where there is no pond or running water. This is called a dry landscape. This kind of dry landscape is to be found at the foot of a mountain, or when one wants to furnish the area between hill and plain one sets rocks in it."[42] This sounds much like the dry cascade at Saihōji, which is often seen as the ultimate example of *karesansui* as described in the *Sakuteiki*. (Musō's work there is also regarded as repre-senting a break with the tradition, by inaugurating dry landscape as an independent style.) A look at this classic treatise, about one quarter of which is devoted to the topic of rocks, will help us better understand their role in the Japanese art of garden making.

The *Sakuteiki* begins on a note of stone:

When arranging rocks [in a garden], it is first and foremost necessary to grasp the overall sense.

Following the topography of the site and seeing how the pond lies, one must think over the particular aesthetic mood [*fuzei*] of all parts of the place. Then recall landscape scenery as it is found in nature [*shōtoku no sansui*], and—taking the variety of different parts into account—arrange the rocks by combining these impressions.

Take as a model the creations left to us by the masters of ancient times; and, considering the suggestions of the owner [of the garden], you should create by exercising your own aesthetic sense [*fuzei*].

Think of the famous places of scenic beauty in the provinces, and mentally absorb what is attractive about them. The general air of these places must be recreated by modeling their attractive features.[43]

The garden maker must first of all cultivate a sense of the *genius loci*, acquire a sound "feeling for the place." The components of the term *fuzei,* which is used frequently in the *Sakuteiki* and later treatises, mean literally "wind" and "feeling." It thus refers equally to the atmosphere or appearance of the place and to the aesthetic feeling or emotion inspired in the viewer.

The garden maker is encouraged to recall natural land-scapes, and indeed the most beautiful among them, in order to understand how something comparable could be effected in the particular site for the garden. The idea is that nature is already a consummate artist, even though we may have to cultivate our sensibility and modify our customary perspective in order to fully appreciate this. There is also an injunction to follow the example of the great figures in the traditional art of the garden, and adapt what one learns from them to the current task. These are two salient features of the East Asian arts generally, where one follows both nature and tradition so as to make a creative contribution in the present. The garden maker is thus supposed to institute two kinds of movement: one in space, whereby the beauty of famous scenic places is invoked in the specific garden, and another in time, whereby the beauty of famous gardens of the past is emulated in the present site.[44]

The opening words of the *Sakuteiki*, "*Ishi o tate . . . ,*" literally mean "When placing rocks," but this locution eventually acquired the broader sense of "When making a garden," which demonstrates the centrality of rock arranging to the development of that art in Japan. The primary principle to be observed is exemplified in the frequent occurrences of the locution *kowan ni shitagau,* which means "following the request [of the rock]." It is used to encourage a responsiveness on the part of the garden maker to what we might call the "soul" of the stone: the translator refers in this context to the Japanese term *ishigokoro,* meaning the "heart," or "mind," of the rock.[45] Rather than imposing a preconceived design onto the site and the elements to be arranged there, the accomplished garden maker will be sensitive to what the particular rocks "want." If he listens carefully, they will tell him where they best belong.

For example, under the heading of "Oral Instructions concerning the Placing of Rocks," the reader (listener) is advised to position first the "master rock" with its distinct character, and then "proceed to set the other rocks in compliance with the 'requesting mood' of the Master Rock."[46] The vocabulary of rock arranging was quite sophisticated by the time the *Sakuteiki* was written, as evidenced by the large number of terms of art applied to different kinds of stone in this short text. They range from the ordinary: such as *waki-ishi* (side rock) and *fuse-ishi* (lying rock); through specialized terms used in connection with ponds, streams, and waterfalls: such as *namikae-ishi* (wave-repelling rock), *mizu-kiri-no-ishi* (water-cutting rock), and *tsutai-ishi* (stepping stone); to the unusual: *shu-ishi* (master rock), *sanzon-seki* (Buddhist triad rocks), *ishigami* (demon rock), and *ryōseki* (rock of vengeful spirits).

A passage containing advice concerning the arrangement of rocks at the foot of hillsides assimilates them to the animal realm: they should be placed in such a way as to resemble "a pack of dogs crouching on the ground, or a running and scattering group of pigs, or else calves playing beside a recumbent mother cow." The theriomorphism gives way to personification: "In general, for one or two 'running away' rocks one should place seven or eight 'chasing rocks.'

The rocks may thus resemble, for example, children playing a game of tag." The dyad of "running" and "chasing" is
followed by several others: "For the leaning rock there is the
supporting rock, for the trampling rock the trampled, for the
looking-up rock there is the looking-down one, and for the
upright the recumbent."[47]

Another passage, in a narrative that may have its source
in the Chinese tradition, likens the rocks to more exalted
human beings. "One theory says that the mountain symbolizes the king, and water his subjects, whereas the rocks represent the king's counselors. . . . The weakness of the mountain occurs when there are no supporting rocks, just as the
king is vulnerable when he has no retainers serving as his
counselors." There are numerous references to ideas from
*fengshui,* mostly in connection with the orientation and
flow of streams, but in the case of waterfalls and the rocks
around them the imagery is drawn from Esoteric Buddhism.
"Achala (the divine Fudō-Myōō) avowed that any waterfall
reaching a height of three feet represents his body. . . . [Rocks
in] tall waterfalls always take the form of the Buddhist triad,
in which the two front rocks to the right and left represent
the two attendants of the celestial family of Achala."[48]
Buddhist iconography often has the god Fudō standing in
front of a waterfall, and it has been argued that when the
*Sakuteiki* speaks of "natural landscape scenery" this already
includes landscape scenery "depicted in paintings."[49] It is
interesting to note that in sculptural representations of Fudō
he is a motionless (though vital) figure surrounded by an

aureole of wildly licking flames—the perfect antithesis of his manifestation in a garden as a fall of water against a background of solid rock.

There is a substantial section of the *Sakuteiki* entitled "Taboos on the Placing of Rocks," which is full of warnings against violating taboos deriving from *fengshui* practices. But a primary prohibition appears to be grounded more generally in a reluctance (not so evident in the Chinese treatises) to infringe upon naturalness.

Placing sideways a rock that was originally vertical, or setting up vertically one that was originally lying, is taboo. If this taboo is violated, the rock will surely turn into a "rock of vengeful spirits" and will bring a curse. Do not place any rock as tall as four or five feet to the northeast of the estate. A rock so placed may become fraught with vengeful spirits, or else may afford a foothold for evil to enter, with the result that the owner will not dwell there for long. However, if the spirits of such a rock are opposed by Buddhist triad rocks set to the southeast corner of the site, evil karma will not gain entry.[50]

There is a combination of considerations here drawn from *fengshui* (the northeast as the most inauspicious direction) and Buddhism. The author cites a Song dynasty writer who says that in cases where rocks have ended up in a different orientation as a result of having fallen down the mountainside, these may be positioned in the latter way "because the change was effected not by human being but by nature." But in some provinces of Japan, the author warns, certain rocks may become demonic simply by being moved. Some configurations are to be avoided because they resemble the forms of Chinese characters with inauspicious meanings (such as the graph for "curse"), while others are to be encouraged for the opposite reason (as with a pattern of three rocks resembling the graph for "goods"—Jpn., *shina*).[51]

The misfortunes that will beset the master of the house if taboos are violated are various: he may lose the property, be plagued by illnesses (including skin diseases and epidemics), suffer harm from outsiders, and so forth. Even the women of the household will be adversely affected by transgressions in the layout, as when a valley between hills points toward the house.

A later treatise on gardens, *Sansui narabini yakeizu* (Illustrations of landscape scenes and ground forms), dates from the fifteenth century and bears the name of a Zen priest, Zōen, as its author. Whereas the *Sakuteiki* deals with Heian-period pleasure gardens from the point of view of the aristocratic owner, the *Sansui* manual is based on the experience of workmen "in the field," and treats much smaller mediaeval gardens designed to be viewed from the building to which they are adjacent—the so-called "contemplation gardens" (*kanshō-niwa*).[52] About one half of the text is devoted to the topic of rock arrangement.

Whereas the *Sakuteiki* eschews the use of proper names for rocks, the *Sansui* manual speaks in Confucian terms of Master and Attendant Rocks: "The Master Rock looks after its Attendants, and the Attendant Rocks look up to the Master." The Attendant Rocks are "flat-topped rocks, resembling persons with their heads lowered, respectfully saying something to the Master Rock." Of similar Confucian origin are the "Respect and Affection Rocks," which are "two stones set slightly apart with their brows inclined toward one another," which are said later in the text to "create the impression of a man and a woman engaged in intimate conversation." Aside from appellations deriving from the Confucian tradition, another section in the *Sansui* manual with the heading "Names of Rocks" lists dozens of names from the Daoist, Buddhist, and Shinto traditions (the "Rock of the Spirit Kings," "Twofold World Rocks," "Torii Rocks" and so forth).[53] The *Sansui* manual again issues warnings against breaking taboos, especially by reversing the "natural" or "original" position of a rock, which will "anger its spirit and bring bad luck."[54]

By contrast with the *Sakuteiki,* the later manual is richly illustrated, with numerous drawings and sketches. The brushwork suggests influence from Song style landscape painting, which was being much imitated in Japan at the time, and some of the techniques and ideas about composing "garden views" and *keiseki* groups (depicting scenery in condensed form) may well be based on Song landscape theories.[55]

One of the most famous Japanese gardens to be influenced by Song landscape painting is the second masterpiece attributed to Musō Soseki, the garden at Tenryūji. On the far side of the pond from the main building there is a dry cascade. Although consisting of fewer elements than its precursor at Saihōji, it comprises much larger rocks of equally exquisite shape, which are again weathered with bands of lichen that suggest downflowing water. In view of the more open nature of this site—the garden at Tenryūji is a beautiful example of *shakkei,* or "borrowed landscape," where the composition is designed to include natural landscape beyond the garden— the luxuriant vegetation around the rocks accentuates their stark minerality. Again in contrast with the upper garden of Saihōji, it is also a consummate example of *shukkei,* or "concentrated scenery," in which a vast scene is compressed into a small space in the manner of a Song dynasty landscape painting.

Although their minerality is set into relief by the surrounding plant life, the rocks that make up the dry cascade look anything but lifeless. Nor is what animates them the minimal accommodation, on the part of these beings that have never known life or death, of the simplest life-forms, lichen and moss. The longer one contemplates them, the more alive they appear with a life all their own. In the course of the sermon that Musō gave at Tenryūji on becoming its founding abbot, he emphasized that the Buddha Dharma (which means both "teachings" and "law") is to be found not only in sacred scriptures but also in the physical world around us. "Everything the world contains— grasses and trees, bricks and tile, all creatures, all actions and activities—are nothing but the manifestations of [the Buddha] Dharma [*hō*]. Therefore it is said that all phenomena in the universe bear the mark of this Dharma. . . . Every single person here is precious in himself, and everything here—plaques, paintings, square eaves and round pillars—

every single thing is preaching the Dharma."[56] Musō is speaking here from a venerable tradition of Japanese Buddhist thinking about the natural world (to be discussed in the last section). The idea that all things expound the Dharma (*hosshin seppō*) is central to Kūkai's Shingon School of esoteric Buddhism, and Zen master Dōgen is fond of insisting that "tiles and pebbles" are "Buddha-nature" (*busshō*) just as much as so-called "sentient" beings are.[57]

Even though the garden is designed to be viewed as a scroll painting from the verandah of the main building, it is a pity that visitors are no longer allowed to take the path that borders the pond around to the far side, so as to be able to see the rocks of the dry cascade at closer quarters. Nevertheless the distant view allows one to appreciate the most significant contribution of the site at Tenryūji, which is the mirroring effect of the pond. Only on a very windy day can one contemplate the waterless fall of rocks without being aware of its being "doubled" by the reflections in the pool at its base. The substantial rocks, which seem to descend majestically down the hillside, harboring an invisible cascade, are mirrored by insubstantial inverted counterparts beneath them. But rather than suggesting a contrast between the real and the illusory, the juxtaposition of rocks and reflections somehow evokes an interplay on the *same* ontological level. The natural world and its image, the substantial and its opposite, are both there at the same time. They are both necessary, belonging together: the point is simply to distinguish between them, which one can only do by acknowledg-

ing the insubstantial counterpart even when—or especially
when—it is not directly presented in a mirror image.


## Stone in the Western Tradition

The Chinese and Japanese understandings of stone considered so far will appear, to a traditional Western perspective
informed by Cartesian dualism, as "primitive animism" or,
at the very least, crude anthropomorphism. But such a view
itself comes from a limited and parochial standpoint. Since
Cartesian dualism deflated the "world soul" of antiquity,
draining the *anima mundi,* as it were, and confining all soul
to a locus within human beings alone, then any apparent
animation of nonhuman phenomena must be seen as a result
of anthropomorphic projection. The perspective is parochial
in view of the widespread reverence for rocks in most other
parts of the world. (The Australian aboriginal, Polynesian,
and Native American traditions come immediately to mind,
but respect for stone seems to come naturally for indigenous
cultures.) For those of us that do not subscribe to Cartesian
dualism, some such term as "panpsychism" might better
denote world views that see humans on an unbroken continuum of "animateness" with natural phenomena. This is not
to deny that the Cartesian perspective, insofar as it enabled
the development of modern technology, has brought many
benefits: it is simply to point out that it is only one perspective among many, however practically efficacious it may be.

It is also a perspective that, through emphasizing our separateness and difference from the natural world, conduces to environmental degradation—and in part by obscuring our participation in the mineral realm.

The biblical passages mentioned by François Berthier concerning the nourishing capacities of stone and the taboo against profaning its naturalness are atypical with respect to the Western tradition in general. The very beginnings of that tradition, philosophically, suggest some parallels with Chinese ideas, but the mainstream soon diverges. Thales, "father of Western philosophy," is believed to have said that "the entire universe is ensouled," supposedly on the basis of the dynamic qualities of the Magnesian stone and amber. (Remember how Guo Pu, father of Chinese geomancy, was also fascinated by the properties of amber and the lodestone.) Aristotle remarks that none of his predecessors associated soul with the element of earth, perhaps because of the assumption that "movement is the distinctive characteristic of soul."[58] This assumption seems pervasive in the Western traditions, presumably because—except for those who live in regions subject to earthquakes or volcanic eruptions— the movements of earth are difficult to perceive in the short term. While Aristotle was reluctant to attribute soul to what we now call inanimate nature, he did claim that plants are ensouled, and that humans too are animated by the same "nutritive and generative" features of the vegetal soul.

Subsequent Western thinkers have been similarly reluctant to regard the mineral realm as animate, with the exception of a few magically or alchemically inclined philosophers during the Renaissance. However, certain strains in the Judaic tradition constitute another exception to the general lack of respect for rock. "Rock" is often used as an epithet for Yahweh Himself, to suggest qualities of steadfastness and stability. Martin Buber cites an old Hasid master who said: "When you walk across the fields with your mind pure and holy, then from all the stones, and all growing things, and all animals, the sparks of their soul come out and cling to you, and then they are purified and become a holy fire in you."[59] It may be thanks to the heretical Spinoza that certain elements from this tradition find their way into some post-Romantic attitudes toward the mineral realm. Spinoza's "pantheistic" notion of the divinity of the whole of nature (*deus sive natura*) was a major influence on a figure who stands at the beginning of an important heterodox line of thinking about rock: namely, Goethe, who had a great interest in geology and mineralogy. In a fragmentary but fascinating piece entitled "On Granite," Goethe explains why "the presence of rock brings elation and assurance to [his] soul."[60]

Near the beginning of this unfinished essay, Goethe remarks with satisfaction that "the ancient insight that granite is the highest and the deepest" is confirmed by "every foray into unknown mountains": "It reposes unshakably in the deepest entrails of the earth, at the same time as its high ridges soar upward, in peaks never reached by the all-surrounding waters." Against the common assumption of a contradiction between the human heart as "the youngest, most multifaceted, dynamic, changeable, and susceptible part of creation," and rock as "the oldest, most solid, deep, and unshakable son of nature," Goethe maintains that "all natural phenomena stand in precise connection with each other." Sitting on a high peak of exposed granite, surveying a vast panorama, he addresses himself as follows: "Here you rest immediately upon a ground that reaches down to the deepest parts of the earth, and no younger stratum, no agglomerated alluvial debris have interposed themselves between you and the solid floor of the archaic world. By contrast with those beautiful and fruitful valleys where you walk on a perpetual grave, these peaks have never produced anything living nor consumed anything living, being prior to all life and above all life." Goethe emphasizes the intimate connection between soul and stone—and at the same time redeems rock from the realm of the dead or lifeless. And when, inspired by granite, he writes of "the sublime tranquillity granted by the solitary and mute nearness of great, soft-voiced nature," he echoes, perhaps unwittingly, East Asian understandings of stone.

Goethe's ideas influenced American transcendentalism, and they are perhaps a factor in the more open attitude toward the mineral world that one finds in Emerson and Thoreau. In a journal entry written while he was in his mid-thirties, Emerson records a kind of death experience he underwent on walking out of the house into a night lit by the full moon. "In the instant you leave behind all human relations . . . and live only with the savages—water, air, light, carbon, lime, & granite. . . . I become a moist, cold element. 'Nature grows over me.' . . . I have died out of the human world & come to feel a strange, cold, aqueous, terr-

aqueous, aerial, ethereal sympathy and existence."[61] The
early Emerson is constantly impressed by "the moral influence of nature upon every individual," which he understands
as "that amount of truth which it illustrates to him": "Who
can estimate this?" he asks; "Who can guess how much
firmness the sea-beaten rock has taught the fisherman?"
Like Goethe a great believer in the ancient principle that
"like can only be known by like," Emerson thinks that the
sea-beaten rock can teach the fisherman firmness because
it speaks to a rocklike solidity deep within the human
soul. This would be the basis for "that spirit which suffices
quiet hearts, which seems to come forth to such from every
dry knoll of sere grass, from every pine-stump, and half-
imbedded stone, on which the dull March sun shines."[62]

Emerson was one of the first thinkers to appreciate
the changes that the then new science of geology was effect-
ing in our understanding of the world. Having invoked in his
essay "Nature" the "patient periods that must round themselves before the rock is formed, and the first lichen race has
disintegrated the thinnest external plate into soil," he writes:
"It is a long way from granite to the oyster; farther yet to Plato,
and the preaching of the immortality of the soul."[63] Long
though the way is, it does not leave the granite behind, which
persists within, allowing the human soul to participate in the
deathlessness as well as the mortality of the natural world.

In our Faustian drive to order the physical world
outside us, it is imprudent to ignore the inner world. In a
passage from the essay "Fate," which influenced Nietzsche's
emphasis on the need for self-discipline and self-cultivation

(and is remarkably consonant with the role of this kind of practice in the East Asian traditions), Emerson writes: "On one side, elemental order, sandstone and granite, rock-ledges, peat-bog, forest, sea and shore; and, on the other part, thought, the spirit which composes and decomposes nature,—here they are, side by side, god and devil, mind and matter, king and conspirator, belt and spasm, riding peacefully together in the eye and brain of every man." And just as the Zen Buddhist thinkers urge us to acknowledge our interdependence with natural phenomena, so Emerson offers near the end of his career a similar exhortation, when he writes: "See what a cometary train of auxiliaries man carries with him, of animals, plants, stones, gases, and imponderable elements. Let us infer his ends from this pomp of means."[64]

As Emerson moved away from the Christian and Neoplatonic ideas that informed his earlier thinking about nature, his stance became steadily less anthropocentric and more consonant with the non-Western philosophies in which he became gradually more interested. His younger friend Henry David Thoreau devoted a larger proportion of his energies to thinking about nature, and began from a less anthropocentric starting point than his mentor had done. Although Thoreau's reading in Chinese thought appears to have focused on the Confucian classics, his profound reverence for nature reduces anthropocentrism close to the minimum that is characteristic of Daoist thought. A passage describing sailing down the Merrimack River echoes the emphasis on fluidity that one finds in the *Daodejing* attributed to Laozi. "All things seemed with us to flow. . . . The hardest material seemed to obey the same law with the most fluid, and so indeed in the long run it does. . . . There were rivers of rock on the surface of the earth, and rivers of ore in its bowels, and our thoughts flowed and circulated, and this portion of time was the current hour."[65]

Although his familiarity with Asian thought did not extend to Japan, Thoreau shares the Japanese Buddhists' appreciation of nature as a source of wisdom. Just as the duke in Shakespeare's *As You Like It* found "sermons in stones and books in the running brooks," so Emerson maintained that "all things with which we deal, preach to us." Now Thoreau emphasizes nature as a scripture that can be read: "The skies are constantly turning a new page to view. The wind sets the types on this blue ground, and the inquiring may always read a new truth there." And while he was an avid reader of literature (he took his Homer with him to Walden Pond), Thoreau warns that if we concentrate too much on reading "particular written languages, which are themselves but dialects and provincial, we are in danger of forgetting the language which all things and events speak without metaphor, which alone is copious and standard."[66]

Just as the East Asian thinkers undermined the distinction between sentient and nonsentient beings, so Thoreau extended the domain of the organic into the so-called "inanimate" world. A well-known passage from *Walden* reads: "There is nothing inorganic. . . . The earth is not a mere fragment of dead history . . . but living poetry like the leaves of a tree, which precede flowers and fruit—not a fossil earth, but a living earth; compared with whose great central life all animal and vegetable life is merely parasitic."[67] Thoreau's emphasis on the vitality of the mineral realm serves to mitigate the effects not only of anthropocentrism but also of biocentrism, in a way that anticipates contemporary "ecocentric" thinking. This line of thought leads on to figures like Aldo Leopold, who expanded the notion of community to include the earth, as a basis for formulating a "land ethic."

Goethe's ideas were the source of a parallel (though largely ignored) current of thinking in Germany, through his influence on Schopenhauer and Nietzsche. Schopenhauer recommends careful consideration of the inorganic world, and suggests that we reflect on such phenomena as "the powerful, irresistible impulse with which masses of water rush downwards, the persistence and determination with which the magnet always turns back to the North Pole, the keen desire with which iron flies to the magnet, and the vehemence with which the poles of the electric current strive for reunion." If we contemplate further "the rapid formation of the crystal with such regularity of configuration," and feel how "a burden, which hampers a body by its gravitation toward the earth, incessantly presses and squeezes this body in pursuit of its one tendency," we will understand that the inorganic realm is animated by the same "will" that energizes us, only at a lower degree of "objectification" than in the case of plants, animals, and humans. It is interesting that Schopenhauer should mention in this context the *yin* and *yang* philosophy found in the Chinese classic on change

(*Yijing*).[68] But the thinker who is perhaps most at home with the idea of our closeness to stone and the inorganic world is Nietzsche, whose understanding of nature was also deeply influenced by Emerson.[69]

With reference to the inorganic as the supposedly "dead world," Nietzsche writes (in the spirit of Goethe): "Let us beware of saying that life is opposed to death. The living is merely a species of the dead, and a very rare species at that." He then expresses the hope that human beings will be able to *naturalize* themselves after having "de-divinized" nature. What such a naturalization might involve is suggested by a brief aphorism from the same period with the title, "How one is to turn to stone." It reads: "Slowly, slowly to become hard like a precious stone—and finally to lie there still, and to the joy of eternity."[70]

A hint of how a human being might "turn to stone" is in turn derivable from several unpublished notes from this period, which evidence a fascination with the benefits of participation in the world of the inorganic. The following resolution, with its slight Buddhist tinge, exemplifies an apt attitude for viewing Zen gardens: "To procure the advantages of one who is dead . . . to think oneself away out of humanity, to unlearn desires of all kinds: and to employ the entire abundance of one's powers in *looking.*" And yet this unlearning of desires need not make existence in any way dull: "To be released from life and become dead nature again can be experienced as a *festival*—of the one who wants to die. To love nature! Again to revere what is dead!" We are able to "become dead nature again" thanks to our physical constitution as living organisms: "How distant and superior is our attitude toward what is dead, the anorganic, and all the while we are three-quarters water and have anorganic minerals in us that perhaps do more for our well- and ill-being than the whole of living society! . . . The inorganic conditions us through and through: water, air, earth, the shape of the ground, electricity, etc."[71] Thanks to such conditioning—which is precisely the topic of *fengshui*—we can realize our participation in the mineral realm, which is the ground of our feeling of familiarity with rocks.

In *Beyond Good and Evil* Nietzsche writes of the way that learning transforms us, as nourishment does, but then adds: "But in our very ground, 'deep down,' there is admittedly something unteachable, a granite of spiritual fate." The Japanese philosopher Nishitani Keiji connects this statement with Goethe's essay on granite, and with the idea of something similarly unchanging deep within the human soul.[72] Stone always held a special significance for Nietzsche: several significant childhood memories have to do with "digging up calcite" and other rocks on a ridge near his home. He even alludes to a language of stone when he asks, clearly referring to himself: "Is a human being not well described when we hear that . . . from childhood on he experiences and reveres unhewn rocks as witnesses of prehistory which are eager to acquire language . . . ?" And the thought of "the eternal recurrence of the same," which he regarded as the pinnacle of his thinking and "the highest formula of affirmation that is attainable," first struck him near a magnificent pyramidal rock on the shore of a lake in the Upper Engadin in Switzerland.[73] The thought that enables the greatest affirmation of life strikes the thinker as he stands by a pyramid-shaped rock, which is "prior to and superior to all life."

It is not generally known that Nietzsche's friendship with the Japanophile Reinhard von Seydlitz, who was a great connoisseur of Japanese art, instilled in him a desire to emigrate to Japan. "If only I were in better health and had sufficient income," he wrote to his sister in 1885, "I would, simply in order to attain greater serenity, emigrate to *Japan.*... I like being in Venice because things could be somewhat Japanese there—a few of the necessary conditions are in place."[74] One of the things very much in place there is the subject celebrated in John Ruskin's classic, *The Stones of Venice* (1853), a book that Nietzsche would have appreciated. But if he had fulfilled his fantasy of emigrating to Japan, Nietzsche would surely have found the Zen rock gardens there conducive to even greater serenity.

We have discovered in the ideas of these exceptional appreciators of stone in the West a theme that we shall see developed and amplified in Japanese Buddhist philosophy: the idea that if we attend to the "great central life" of the earth we shall hear some teachings and see some scriptures couched and proclaimed in a language of nature's own—and in an unexpected eloquence of stone.

## Cutting out Dry Landscapes

The best way to approach the rock garden at Ryōanji—a later example of the *karesansui* style, and for many its highest consummation—is *slowly,* deviating from what is nowadays helpfully signposted as the "Usual Route." It is such a relief to leave behind the commotion of traffic and bustle of the city, and walk up the cobblestone pathway leading from the street, that one is inclined to head for the famous site directly. But the grounds of the temple as a whole are exquisite, and one could easily spend a day admiring the ponds, rocks, trees, and other vegetation that make up the environs of the dry landscape garden.

To let the rock garden exert its most powerful effect, one does well to experience its context (something to which Buddhist philosophy is always sensitive) by contemplating beforehand the rich profusion of natural—though also arranged—beauty that surrounds it. In numerous sub-gardens handsome rocks stand among elegant trees and bushes, while others lie, apparently slumbering, in sun-illumined moss that glows green around them. Majestic stands of bamboo sway in the breeze, as if beckoning to shadowy backgrounds. Exotic palms thrust sharply skyward among trees that blossom delicately in the spring. Such profusion intensifies the eventual encounter with the distinct *lack* of profusion at the heart of these gardens, which the philosopher Hisamatsu Shin'ichi has suggested should be called "garden of emptiness" (*kūtei*) rather than "rock garden" (*sekitei*).[75]

Getting back to the "Usual Route": on climbing the broad and gradual gradient of the steps that lead up to the buildings surrounding the rock garden, one might notice underfoot a variety of exquisitely colored cobblestones. And if the male visitor happens to pay a visit to the appropriate facilities before viewing the garden, he can enjoy from the window a unique preliminary perspective, through an opening in the garden wall, on the group of rocks nearest the far end. (I am assured that the angle of vision from the window of the women's facilities does not, unfortunately, afford a similar perspective.) This is the time for the returning viewer to prepare to be astonished, on first stepping onto the wooden walkway that runs along the north side, at how small the garden is in area. Although it measures less than thirty meters from east to west and ten from north to south, one tends to remember it as being much larger than it really is. (At least in my own case, in spite of mental preparation each time, I never fail to be amazed upon first seeing it again: its image in memory remains persistently vast.)

At first glance a profound stillness seems to reign within the frame of the garden, a peace that contrasts at busy times with the hubbub on the walkway and, formerly, with the taped and loudspeakered announcements that used to proclaim the place as "the garden of emptiness." There is also an overwhelming impression, initially, of sparse sterility—until one notices the moss that surrounds several of the rocks and the thin layer of lichen on some of them. Not much life for a garden, admittedly, but just enough, insofar as it provides a striking contrast to the unremittingly inorganic nature of the rest. In summer the bright green of the moss echoes the lush colors of the trees, while in winter its darker greens and mauves match the hues of both the evergreens and the bare branches of the deciduous trees that border the wall. Being surrounded by a sea of gray gravel, the moss emphasizes the effect created by the elements of the garden being "cut off" from the nature outside. Without these touches of green life the place would look quite different—just as the "seed" of white within the black part of the yin-yang figure (and vice versa) perfects the pattern.

The "cutoff" is effected by the magnificent wall that runs the length of the garden and around the west side. The wall is a work of art in itself, though inadvertently so: thanks to its having been made of clay boiled in oil, fantastic patterns have emerged over the centuries as the oil has gradually seeped out. Throughout most of its length, mysterious landscapes have appeared on the wall's vertical face, suggesting mist-veiled depths, and its exquisitely weathered hues complement the colors of the rocks and moss it encloses. They are like Song landscapes on a horizontal scroll. The "skies" of these landscape paintings are cut off by a shingled roof running along the wall's length, the angle of which (at around 45°) mediates perfectly between the interior space of the garden and the world outside. The wall thus exemplifies a technique known in Japanese aesthetic discourse as *kire-tsuzuki,* or "cut-continuance."[76]

The topos of the cut derives from Zen Buddhist thinking. The Rinzai master Hakuin urged his students to "cut off the root of life" through giving up the idea that the self is real, so that they can then "return to life" with renewed energies. There is a minor instance of this cut in the life-sustaining process of breathing: the moment between exhalation and inhalation, between contraction and expansion, is a moment of "cut-continuance" (at least until the final cut when one breathes one's last). Another exemplification is to be found in haiku poetry, which often employs what is called the *kireji,* or "cutting syllable," which effects a cut at the end of a line—and at the same time links it to the next. A consummate example occurs in one of Bashō's best known poems, which begins

Furuike ya
(An ancient pond — )

and where the *ya* at the end of the first line is a syllable that "cuts" to the next line—in much the same way as a director cuts from one scene to the next in a film, breaking and maintaining continuity at the same time.

At Ryōanji the wall cuts the rock garden off from the outside—and yet is low enough to permit a view of that outside from the viewing platform. This cut (which is itself double because of the angled roof that runs along the top of the wall) is most evident in the contrast between movement and stillness. Above the wall one sees nature in movement: branches wave and sway, clouds float by, and the occasional bird flies past—though hardly ever, it seems, *over* the garden proper. Within the garden's borders (unless rain or snow is falling, or a stray leaf is blown across) the only visible movement is shadowed or illusory. In seasons when the sun is low, shadows of branches move slowly across the sea of gravel. This movement tends to accentuate the stillness of the rocks—to the point where even in its absence the rocks themselves seem to be on the move, to be in some sense "underway."

The garden is cut off on the near side too, by a border of pebbles larger, darker, and more rounded than the pieces of gravel, which runs along the east and north edges. There is a striking contrast between the severe rectangularity of the garden's borders and the irregular natural forms of the rocks within them. On closer inspection the border on the east side turns out to have a right-angled kink in it, as if disrupted by the powerful presence of the large group of rocks adjacent to it (see figure 16, above). The expanse of gravel is also cut through by the upthrust of the rocks from below, earth energies mounting and peaking in irruptions of stone. Each group of rocks is cut off from the others by the expanse of gravel, the separation being enhanced by the ripple patterns in the raking that surrounds each group (and some individual rocks). And yet the overall effect is to intensify the invisible lines of connection among the rocks, whose interrelations exemplify the fundamental Buddhist insight of "dependent co-arising."

A related and more radical cut is to be found in the distinctively Japanese art of flower arrangement called *ikebana*. The term means literally "making flowers live"— a strange name, on first impression at least, for an art that begins by killing them. There is an exquisite essay by Nishitani Keiji on this marvelous art, in which the life of one of the most beautiful kinds of natural being is cut off, precisely in order to let the true nature of that being come to the fore.[77] There is something curiously deceptive, from the Buddhist viewpoint of the impermanence of all things, about plants, insofar as they sink roots into the earth. In severing the flowers from their roots, Nishitani argues, and placing them in an alcove, one lets them show themselves as they really are: as absolutely rootless as every other being in this world of radical impermanence.

Something similar is going on in the rock garden, insofar as the cutoff from the surrounding nature has the effect of *drying up* its organic life, which then no longer decays in the usual manner. *Karesansui* means, literally, "dried up" or "withered" mountains and waters, but when Musō writes the word in the title of his *Ode to the Dry Landscape* he uses a different graph for the *kare* with the meaning "provisional," or "temporary." Being dried up, the mountains and waters of the garden at Ryōanji appear less temporary than their counterparts outside, which manifest the cyclical changes that natural life is heir to. But just as plants look deceptively permanent thanks to their being rooted in the earth, so the impression of permanence given by the rocks of the dry landscape garden—especially strong for the visitor who returns decade after decade, each time feeling (and looking) distinctly more impermanent—is nevertheless misleading. They too shall pass away.

The rocks and gravel are not real mountains and waters: they are just rocks and gravel, even though they are arranged *like* a landscape. Nishitani has emphasized the significance of this "like"ness (*nyo*) in Zen, where each thing, thanks to its oneness with emptiness, is "an image without an original," and thus "like" itself alone.[78] The last stanza of a poem by Dōgen, called "The Point of Zazen," reads:

The water is clean, right down to the ground,
Fishes are swimming like (*nyo*) fishes.
The sky is wide, clear through to the heavens,
And birds are flying like (*nyo*) birds.[79]

The *nyo* here is the Japanese equivalent for the Buddhist term "suchness": in its oneness with emptiness, a being is what it is in being like what it is, in its "just-like-this-ness." The rocks and gravel at Ryōanji, in being like mountains and waters but cut off from nature and dried up, conceal the mutable outward form of natural phenomena and thereby reveal their true form: suchness, as being one with emptiness. More concretely, Nishitani has explained their enigmatic power in terms of their ability to enlighten and teach. "We are within the garden and are not just spectators, for we have ourselves become part of the actual manifestation of the garden architect's expression of his own enlightenment experience. The garden is my Zen master now, and it is your Zen master too."[80] In a chapter of his major work entitled "Voices of the River Valley, Shapes of the Mountain," Dōgen writes that while we are seeking a teacher, one may "spring out from the earth" and "make nonsentient beings speak the truth."

It might also help to recall here the well-known description of the course of Zen practice by the Chinese master Qingyuan Weixin: "When I had not yet begun to study Zen thirty years ago, I thought that mountains are mountains and waters are waters. Later when I studied with my master, I entered realization and understood that mountains are not mountains, waters are not waters. Now that I abide in the way of no-seeking, I see as before that mountains are just mountains, waters are just waters."[81] The second phase brings the realization that mountains and waters are insubstantial, images without originals, manifestations of emptiness and thus commensurable with any other such manifestations. In the final phase they are experienced as "just mountains" and "just waters"—as before, and yet not quite as before, since they are no longer seen from the anthropocentric perspective but rather in their own uniqueness, just as they are in themselves. In the garden at Ryōanji the rocks are *like* mountains (the likeness being especially striking when they are viewed through binoculars or the telephoto lens of a camera) and the gravel is *like* an expanse of water. The rocks are also like animals, and other creatures besides. And yet ultimately the rocks and gravel are just rocks and gravel.

The more one contemplates this remarkable garden, and especially the interrelations among the fifteen rocks and the five groups, the more profoundly right the arrangement appears. The way this work generates a space vibrant with manifold energies has been compared to the famous black ink painting of the six persimmons by Mu Qi.[82] There is much to justify the claim that these two works constitute the consummate expression of profound Buddhist ideas in the arts of East Asia.

But there is an aspect of our aesthetic response to these rock gardens that has received insufficient attention in commentaries hitherto: the sense that the arranged rocks somehow "speak to us." Whereas the aesthetics of Zen rock gardens have been discussed in terms of various concepts and ideas drawn from the Japanese tradition, little has been said about the ontological status of stone as understood in Japanese Buddhism.

## Rocks as Sources of Understanding

In order to dispel the specter of "primitive animism" that tends to haunt any discussions of rock as more than lifeless, I shall focus on the two most sophisticated thinkers in the tradition of Japanese Buddhist philosophy, Kūkai and Dōgen. Their philosophies rank with those of the greatest figures in the Western tradition, from Plato and Augustine to Hegel and Heidegger, though only a brief sketch of the relevant, complex ideas can be given here.[83] Anyone familiar with the profundity of Kūkai or Dōgen knows that whatever their talk of the speech of natural phenomena may mean, it is worlds away from any kind of primitivism.

The Shingon Esoteric School was the first form of Buddhism to influence the development of Japanese gardens, by introducing mandala and other kinds of symbolism into their construction. In several of his writings, the founder of the school, Kūkai (744–835), effects a bold innovation in Mahayana Buddhist thinking by revisioning the Dharmakaya (*hosshin*), which had been previously understood as the formless and timeless Absolute, as the "reality embodiment" of the cosmic Buddha Mahavairochana (Dainichi Nyorai) and nothing other than the physical universe. This means that rocks and stone—indeed all of "the four great elements"—are to be included among sentient beings and revered as constituting the highest body of the Tathagata (*nyorai* in Japanese: "the one come like this").[84]

Moreover, with his idea of *hosshin seppō* ("the Dharmakaya expounds the Dharma") Kūkai claims that the physical world, as the cosmic Buddha's reality embodiment and in the person of Dainichi Nyorai, proclaims the true teachings of Buddhism.[85] But he also emphasizes that Dainichi expounds the Dharma purely "for his own enjoyment" and not for our benefit (there are other embodiments of the Buddha, the Nirmanakaya and the Sambhogakaya, which take care of that). So even though the cosmos may in some indirect sense be "speaking" to us, it is not doing so in any human language. Speech is for Kūkai one of the "three mysteries" or "intimacies" (*sanmitsu*) of Dainichi, and so it takes considerable practice for human beings to be able to hear and understand the teachings of natural phenomena. To the relief of readers who have struggled in vain to comprehend his formidable texts, Kūkai says at one point that "the Esoteric Buddhist teachings are so profound as to defy expression in writing."[86] His teacher in China, Master Huiguo, had told him that "the profound meaning of the esoteric scriptures could be conveyed only through art." Kūkai often maintained that "the medium of painting" was especially effective, but he would also acknowledge the art of the garden.

Almost five centuries later, Dōgen (1200–53) develops some ideas very similar to Kūkai's, though in terms of the Sōtō Zen tradition, of which he is regarded as the founder. Just as Kūkai identifies the Dharmakaya with the phenomenal world, so Dōgen, inspired by the poem of Su Dongpo mentioned earlier, promotes a similar understanding of natural landscape as the body of the Buddha. During his stay at Lushan, Su had experienced an epiphany upon hearing the sounds of a mountain stream flowing through the night. He then wrote the following poem on landscape as the body of the Buddha and the sounds of natural phenomena as an abundance of Buddhist sermons:

The voices of the river valley are his Wide and Long Tongue,
The form of the mountains is nothing other than his Pure Body.
Throughout the night, eighty-four thousand verses.
On a later occasion, how can I tell them to others?

Dōgen cites this poem, which a Chan master authenticated as evidence of Su Dongpo's enlightenment, in the course of an essay urging his readers to hear and read natural landscapes as Buddhist sermons and scriptures.[87]

Philosophically speaking, Dōgen asserts the nonduality of the world of impermanence and the totality of "Buddha-nature" (the idea of *shitsu-u* as *busshō*). Arguing vehemently against the more "biocentric" standpoint of earlier Buddhism, he claims that Buddha-nature is not just sentient beings but also "fences, walls, tiles, and pebbles" (which are much in evidence at Ryōanji). Elsewhere he writes that "rocks and stones, large and small, are the Buddha's own possessions."[88] Corresponding to Kūkai's notion of *hosshin seppō,* Dōgen develops the idea of *mujō seppō,* which emphasizes that even insentient beings expound the true teachings, though in a different way from the sentient. "At the time of right practice," he writes, "the voices and form of river valleys, as well as the form and voices of mountains, generously bestow their eighty-four thousand hymns of praise."[89]

As well as hearing the cosmos as a sermon, one can see, or read, the natural world as scripture. Kūkai writes in one of his poems:

Being painted by brushes of mountains, by ink of oceans,
Heaven and earth are the bindings of a sutra revealing the truth.[90]

Again, it takes time and effort to learn to read this natural text, but the notion of nature as scripture certainly does justice to the sense we often have that there is something "inscribed" in natural phenomena, and in stone especially, something that means something. Similarly for Dōgen, sutras are not restricted to writings contained in scrolls, since the natural world too can be read as sacred scripture. This is the burden of the chapter in the *Shōbōgenzō* entitled "Sansuigyō," or "Mountains and Waters as Sutras." And in another chapter he writes: "The sutras are the entire universe, mountains and rivers and the great earth, plants and trees."[91]

François Berthier talks about the "mute speech" of the rocks at Ryōanji and imagines their "stifled voice," which says little but proclaims their silence while enjoining us not to speak. His original subtitle, *Reading Zen in the Rocks,* suggests that rocks are also inscriptions that can be read as saying something to do with Zen. Our brief consideration of Kūkai and Dōgen suggests that we may better understand the powerful effect of the rocks and gravel at Ryōanji if we take them to be proclaiming the teachings and read them as a sutra revealing the truths of Buddhism. Just as contemplation of dry landscape gardens can enhance one's understanding of Japanese Buddhism, so a sense for the Japanese Buddhist conception of the expressive powers of so-called "inanimate" nature can help us better appreciate the role of rock in the garden inspired by Zen. We can then understand the rocks at Ryōanji as proclaiming the Buddhist teachings of impermanence and dependent co-arising with unparalleled clarity, as exemplifying such notions as suchness and the cut, and as pointing to our "original nature" which may have more rocklike steadfastness to it, at the deepest layers of the self, than we may previously have realized.[92]

We saw how the Chinese tradition reveres rocks for their age and beauty, and for their being vitally expressive of the fundamental energies of the earth on which we live. Japanese Buddhism adds pedagogic and soteric dimensions by inviting us to regard rocks and other natural phenomena as sources of wisdom and companions on the path to deeper understanding. But nowadays the earth itself is as much in need of saving as are its human inhabitants—and is especially in need of being saved *from* its human inhabitants. To this extent there may be practical and not just aesthetic lessons to be learned from our relations with rock, and compelling reasons to attend to what Goethe calls "the mute nearness of great, soft-voiced nature" both inside and beyond the confines of the dry landscape garden.

The garden at Ryōanji makes a brief but significant appearance in one of Ozu Yasujirō's best films, *Late Spring* (1949). The father and daughter are visiting Kyoto, and the relevant scene immediately follows one of the most written-about shots in the film: a still life in their room in the inn, in which a large vase stands in front of an oval-shaped window patterned with shadows of slowly waving bamboo. The scene of the garden consists of eight shots, seven of which show the Ryōanji rocks. Within it are seven cuts.

    After a shot of the three groups at the far (west) end and a closeup of the group of two at that end (as in figure 22, above), the camera angle reverses, and we see the father with his friend—also the father of a daughter—sitting on the wooden platform with the tops of the same two rocks occupying the lower part of the frame. Two rocks and two fathers. Cut to a closeup of the fathers from their left side, with no rocks in view. But in their dark suits, seated as they are in the classic Ozu "overlapping triangles" configuration, leaning forward toward the garden with their arms around knees drawn up toward their chins, they stay still as two rocks—monumental. They talk about how they raise children who then go off to live their own lives. As they invoke cycles of impermanence, they remain motionless except for the occasional nod or turn of the head. Cut to a shot of the far end of the garden similar to the opening one. Then the two fathers again, but seen from farther back, so that we also see the two rocks in the garden they are looking at. Finally two more shots of the garden, three groups of rocks seen from the far end and four seen from the east end. Then cut back to the bedroom in the inn, where father and daughter are packing in preparation for returning to Kamakura.

In their brief conversation by the edge of the garden the two fathers do little more than exchange platitudes about family life—and yet the scene is a profoundly moving expression of the human condition. It gains this effect from the assimilation of the figures of the two men to rocks, which seems to affirm the persistence of the cycles of impermanence. Now that they are on film, those fathers will always, it seems, be sitting there, monumental figures overlooking the celebrated rock garden of emptiness.

If when leaving one follows the walkway that leads around the back of the main building, one passes a famous *tsukubai* (a stone water basin of the type used before attending a tea ceremony) bearing an inscription of four Chinese characters that mean, "All I know is how much is enough."[93] Even though the basin was placed in Ryōanji a century or two after the rock garden was laid out there, the dictum seems apposite. For the true appreciator there is hardly a richer experience of nature-cum-culture to be had; and yet the means employed for the work that engenders such an experience are minimal.

One is well advised to linger again on the way out. It is worthwhile, immediately on leaving the main building, to stop and admire the famous clay wall of the garden from the outside, since it is a work of art in its own right from that perspective too. And again the power of the garden's effect can be enhanced by experiencing its context after, as well as before, the fact. When one views at leisure the luxuriance of the various subgardens of the temple on the way out with the afterimage of the austere rock garden still in mind, one can appreciate the dual "life-and-death" aspect of reality of which Zen philosophy speaks. It is as if one sees in double exposure, as it were, the life- and deathless source from which all things arise and into which they perish at every moment.[94]

The question of whether there is an "enough" to this kind of experience is one that for me remains open. On every visit to Kyoto I resolve to go to Ryōanji and *not* view the rock garden—thinking such a perverse course of action, or non-action, would be very much in the spirit of Zen. But so compelling is the voice of those rocks, so enchanting the language inscribed on that scroll of gravel, so strong the sensuous attraction of the wall and its manifold cutting, that the resolve remains so far impossible to carry out.

Why should this be? For after attaining a sufficient depth of contemplation of the Ryōanji rock garden, one finds that its image persists, ever accessible, in the memory and imagination. One is always sitting, like the two fathers, on the edge of that force-field of a space. Like the rocks.

# NOTES

## Translator's Preface

1. François Berthier, *Le jardin du Ryōanji: Lire le Zen dans les pierres* (Paris, 1997), back cover.

## Reading Zen in the Rocks

1. The idea of nourishing stone can be found in the Bible: "... and with honey from the rock I would satisfy you" (*Psalms* 81:16); "And he made him suck honey from the rock, and oil out of the flinty rock" (*Deuteronomy* 32:13).

2. Compare the way famous sites of the Mediterranean world were reproduced in the gardens of Hadrian's Villa at Tivoli.

3. The "paradises" of the Persian rulers seem like types of mandala-garden, since they were images of the cosmos. But unlike Japanese gardens their composition was regulated by a very strict geometry.

4. The Buddhists at that time believed that 1,500 years after the Buddha entered nirvana—that is, in 1052 CE—the era of the End of the Dharma would begin, in which the world would be plagued by all kinds of curses.

5. The word *hōjō,* which literally means "ten feet square," is a modest

designation for the residence of the abbott of a Zen temple. In fact these apartments, which consist of several spacious rooms, have nothing of the hermit's humble hut about them.

6. Used by the Egyptians, Greeks, and Etruscans, *boustrophedon* writing is distinguished by signs that recall the pattern of furrows traced by oxen in the fields. The lines run alternately from left to right and then from right to left, or vice versa.

7. "The odd number is pleasing to the divine" (Virgil); "Music above all else, and prefer the odd as a consequence" (Verlaine).

8. For example, the Japanese celebrate as propitious the third, fifth, and seventh birthdays of their children.

9. The *arhat,* or "venerable one," is a man that has attained a high degree of wisdom and understanding: a sort of Buddhist saint.

10. Ikkyū Sōjun (1394–1481) was one of Japan's greatest Zen monks, and the only one to re-connect with the tradition of the Chinese eccentrics of the Tang dynasty.

11. A reference to one of the most beautiful poems of Bashō (1644–94), the master of the haiku: "Prevailing silence — / and penetrating the rock / the cicada's cry."

12. *Sansui* in Japanese. The old reading *senzui* also referred to gardens.

13. Note the close filiation between the terms *matsuri* ("religious festival") and *matsurigoto* ("government").

14. Compiled in 712, the *Kojiki* (Notes on ancient facts) contains the essentials of Japanese mythology.

15. In the West there is the exceptional, though exemplary, case of a painter-gardener: Claude Monet, who was as proud of his garden at Giverny as of his best canvases.

16. People have even gone so far as to attribute the garden at Ryōanji to Musō Soseki, who died a century before the temple was founded.

17. To give just one example of the humiliating situation of the *kawaramono,* they were obliged to kneel when they spoke to other people.

18. A capital had to contain five great Zen temples, which were called "the Five Mountains," which is probably an allusion to the Five Sacred Mountains of China.

19. *Bonseki* [literally, "tray rocks" — Tr.] is to *bonsai* [literally, "tray vegetation" — Tr.] what the rock garden is to a garden of plants.

20. Like Kotarō and Hikojirō, Saburō is the name of a *kawaramono*.

21. The sand at the Silver Pavilion is granulated granite gathered from riverbeds. The grains are relatively large (between 5mm and 7mm millimeters in diameter), sand from the seashore being too fine to be shaped.

22. The *Tale of Genji* [(by Lady Murasaki)], which was written at the beginning of the eleventh century, is one of the major monuments of Japanese literature.

23. Not to be confused with the famous imperial villa of Katsura in Kyoto.

### The Role of Rock in the Japanese Dry Landscape Garden

1. The suggestion of the scholar Mirei Shigemori, as cited in Pierre Rambach and Suzanne Rambach, *Gardens of Longevity in China and Japan: The Art of the Stone Raisers,* trans. André Marling (New York, 1987), 180. This book contains some spectacular color photographs of rocks in Chinese gardens.

2. Dōgen, *Shōbōgenzō,* "Keisei-sanshiki" (Voices of the river-valley, shapes of the mountain). Further references to Dōgen will be made simply by the title of the relevant chapter title of his major work, *Shōbō-genzō* (in Ōkubo Dōshū, ed., *Dōgen zenji zenshū,* vol. 1 [Tokyo, 1969–70]). I follow, with occasional modification, the translations by Nishijima and Cross in *Master Dogen's Shobogenzo,* 4 vols, (Woking [Surrey], 1994–99).

3. Kawabata Yasunari, *Beauty and Sadness,* trans. Howard Hibbett (Rutland and Tokyo, 1975), 86–91. (I have changed "stones" to "rocks" in the translation.) On first visiting the dry cascade at Saihōji, I was immediately struck by the similarity with Cézanne's paintings of rocks, and so was intrigued later to find Keiko, in Kawabata's novel, compare comparing its power with that of "Cézanne's painting of the rocky coasts at L'Estaque" (p. 87). Kawabata may not have been familiar with Cézanne's magnificent canvases of rocks and trees at Fontainebleau, which generate an aesthetic mood much closer to that of the dry cascade.

4. Karl Hennig, *Der Karesansui-Garten als Ausdruck der Kultur der Muromachi-Zeit* (Hamburg, 1982), 111–12; also Irmtraud Schaarschmidt-Richter, *Japanese Gardens,* trans. translated by Janet Seligman (New York, 1979), 180.

5. See Rambach, *Gardens of Longevity,* 39.

6. See Loraine Kuck, *The World of the Japanese Garden: From Chinese Origins to Modern Landscape Art* (New York and Tokyo, 1968), 39. Also John Hay, *Kernels of Energy, Bones of Earth: The Rock in Chinese Art* (New York, 1985), 18. Hay's essay in this exhibition catalogue is a magnificent treatment of the role of rock in Chinese culture more generally.

7. Hay, *Kernels of Energy,* 42 and 50.

8. *The Classical Contents of the Mirror of Profound Depths,* cited in Hay, *Kernels of Energy,* 52. The entry on stone is eighty-six-pages long.

9. John Sallis notes the way mountain peaks "gather the elements," although the rest of his erudite study only treats stone as worked, rather than in its natural state. John Sallis, *Stone* (Bloomington, 1994), 16.

10. François Jullien, *The Propensity of Things: Toward a History of Efficacy in China,* trans. Janet Lloyd (New York, 1995), 91–92, with reference to Guo Pu, *Zangshu* (Book of funerals).

11. Guo Pu, *Eulogy to the Lodestone,* cited in Hay, *Kernels of Energy,* 53.

12. See the discussions of rocks in Rolf A. Stein, *The World in Miniature: Container Gardens and Dwellings in Far Eastern Religious Thought,* trans. Phyllis Brooks (Stanford, 1990).

13. Kong Chuan, Introduction to Du Wan's *Yunlin Shipu* (Cloud Forest catalogue), cited in Hay, *Kernels of Energy,* 38.

14. See William R. LaFleur, "Saigyō and the Buddhist Value of Nature," in J. Baird Callicott and Roger T. Ames, eds., *Nature in Asian Traditions of Thought* (Albany, 1989), 183–86, on which the present paragraph is based. (This article originally appeared in two parts in *History of Religions* 13:2 [November 1973]: 93–126, and 13:3 [February 1974]: 227–48.) In an essay in the same volume, Tu Wei-ming discusses the Chinese view of mountains as "ocean waves frozen in time" and rocks as "dynamic processes with their particular configurations of *qi*" ("The Continuity of Being: Chinese Visions of Nature," 74).

15. Zhanran, *Jingang Bi,* as cited in Fung Yu-lan, *A History of Chinese Philosophy,* 2 vols. (Princeton, 1953), 2:385–86.

16. Kuck, *The World of the Japanese Garden,* 45; Edward H. Schafer, *Tu Wan's Stone Catalogue of Cloudy Forest* (Berkeley, 1961), 5.

17. Description by Yuan Xuanzhi, cited in Maggie Keswick, *The Chinese Garden: History, Art & Architecture* (London and New York, 1978), 155.

18. Kuck, *The World of the Japanese Garden,* 19–22.

19. Marco Polo, *The Travels of Marco Polo,* trans. Ronald Latham (London 1972), 127. Some recent historians have called into question Marco Polo's claim to have reached China, but the account of the green rocks sounds convincing, even if it is not firsthand.

20. Schafer, *Tu Wan's Stone Catalogue,* 57 and 59.

21. Hay, *Kernels of Energy,* 19–21.

22. Hay, *Kernels of Energy,* 36.

23. Du Wan, *Yunlin Shipu,* cited in Hay, *Kernels of Energy,* 22. Hay gives a more complete translation of this passage than does Schafer (*Stone Catalogue,* 52–53), whose edition is a "Synopsis" with commentary. Some of this passage also appears, in a different translation, in Rambach, *Gardens of Longevity,* 42.

24. Hay, *Kernels of Energy,* 99f.

25. Hay, *Kernels of Energy,* 84 and note 173.

26. Schafer, *Tu Wan's Stone Catalogue,* 30.

27. Ji Cheng, *The Craft of Gardens,* trans. Alison Hardie (New Haven and London, 1988), 112 and 114.

28. Ji Cheng, *The Craft of Gardens,* 110.

29. Du Wan, *Yunlin Shipu,* cited in Hay, *Kernels of Energy,* 22.

30. Hay, *Kernels of Energy,* 60 and 27.

31. Hay, *Kernels of Energy,* 32. See also Rambach, *Gardens of Longevity,* 78–79, where there is a reproduction of *Mi Fu's Homage to the Rock* from Wang Gai's *Mustard Seed Garden Manual of Painting,* and Hay, *Kernels of Energy,* 33–35, for three other paintings of this subject.

32. Rambach, *Gardens of Longevity,* 26–29.

33. See Keswick, *The Chinese Garden,* 94–96.

34. From the *Record of Hua Yang Palace* by the monk Zi-xui, cited in Keswick, p. 54.

35. Ibid.

36. Cited in Kuck, *The World of the Japanese Garden,* 182.

37. Dōgen, "Keisei-sanshiki."

38. Dōgen, "Mujō seppō" (Nonsentient beings expound the Dharma).

39. Cited in Hennig, *Der Karesansui-Garten,* 195.

40. For details of the disagreement, see Hennig, *Der Karesansui-Garten,* 116–19.

41. Musō Soseki, *Muchū mondō,* cited in Oscar Benl and Horst

Hammitzsch, eds, *Japanische Geisteswelt: Vom Mythus zur Gegenwart* (Baden-Baden, 1956), 158–59. Translation modified in the light of the original and the discussion by Nishitani Keiji in his *Religion and Nothingness,* trans. Jan Van Bragt (Berkeley, 1982), 108.

42. *Sakuteiki,* as cited in Hennig, *Der Karesansui-Garten,* 193 (compare Shimoyama, *Sakuteiki,* 5).

43. Translation modified from Wybe Kuitert's, in his *Themes, Scenes, and Taste in the History of Japanese Garden Art* (Amsterdam, 1988), 55, in the light of the original, in Mori Osamu, *"Sakuteiki" no sekai : Heiancho no teienbi* (Tokyo, 1986), 43.

44. See Augustin Berque, "L'appareillage de l'ici vers l'ailleurs dans les jardins japonais," *Extrême-Orient Extrême-Occident* 22 (2000). Berque argues convincingly that this kind of double movement, in which the elsewhere and elsewhen are invoked in the here and now—*appareillage* means both "installation" and "getting under sail"—is a primary principle of the art of the garden in Japan.

45. Shimoyama, *Sakuteiki,* ix. Yuriko Saito places appropriate emphasis on the importance of "following the request" of the rocks in her essay, "Japanese Gardens: The Art of Improving Nature," *Chanoyu Quarterly* (1996) 83:41–61.

46. *Sakuteiki,* 23.

47. *Sakuteiki,* 24 and 25.

48. *Sakuteiki,* 19 and 16.

49. See Kuitert, *Themes,* 57–58, and note 142.

50. *Sakuteiki,* 26.

51. *Sakuteiki,* 29–30.

52. Kuitert, *Themes,* 137–39.

53. *Sansui narabini yakeizu,* secs. 4, 84, 14, 78, and 31. I follow the translation of the complete work by David A. Slawson in his *Secret Teachings in the Art of Japanese Gardens* (Tokyo and New York, 1987), 142–75. Slawson reads the work's title as *Senzui narabi ni yagyō no zu,* and translates it as *Illustrations for Designing Mountain, Water, and Hillside Field Landscapes.*

54. *Sansui* manual, sec. 12.

55. See Kuitert, *Themes,* 140–44.

56. Musō Soseki, "Sermon at the Opening of Tenryūji," in Ryusaku

Tsunoda et al., eds, *Sources of Japanese Tradition* (New York and London, 1964), 1:252–55.

57. Kūkai, "The Difference between Exoteric and Esoteric Buddhism," in *Kūkai: Major Works,* trans. Yoshito S. Hakeda (New York, 1972), esp. 151–52; Dōgen, "Busshō" (Buddha-nature).

58. Aristotle, *De Anima,* 405b and 404a.

59. Cited in Annie Dillard, *Pilgrim at Tinker Creek* (New York, 1974), 198. See also her lyrical account of the eponymous substance ("lower than metals and minerals . . . occurring beneath salts and earths") in the final section of *Holy the Firm* (New York, 1977).

60. Johann Wolfgang von Goethe, "Über den Granit," in *Werke: Hamburger Ausgabe* (Munich, 1988), 13:253–58. The translations are my own; a freer rendition can be found in *Goethe: The Collected Works,* ed. and trans. Douglas Miller (Princeton, 1988), 12:131–34.

61. Ralph Waldo Emerson, *Journals,* 5:496–97 (1838).

62. Emerson, *Nature,* "Discipline," in *Ralph Waldo Emerson: Essays and Lectures* (New York, 1983), 29; "The Poet," 461. References to Emerson will be to the page numbers of this (Library of America) edition.

63. Emerson, "Nature," *Essays and Lectures,* 546–47.

64. Emerson, "Fate" and "Considerations by the Way," *Essays and Lectures,* 953 (compare Nietzsche, *Beyond Good and Evil,* aphorism 225) and 1080.

65. Henry David Thoreau, *A Week on the Concord and Merrimack Rivers,* "Thursday," in *Henry David Thoreau* (New York, 1985), 269–70. References to Thoreau will be to the page numbers of this (Library of America) edition.

66. Emerson, *Nature,* "Discipline," 29; Thoreau, *A Week,* "Friday," 292; *Walden,* "Sounds," 411.

67. Thoreau, *Walden,* "Spring," 568.

68. Schopenhauer, *The World as Will and Representation,* vol. 1, secs. 23 and 27. My own translation from the original German: *Die Welt als Wille und Vorstellung* (Stuttgart and Frankfurt, 1960).

69. For more detailed discussion, see my essays, "Floods of Life around Granite of Fate: Nietzsche and Emerson as Thinkers of Nature," *ESQ: A Journal of the American Renaissance* 43 (1997): 207–40, and "Staying Loyal to the Earth: Nietzsche as an Ecological Thinker," in John Lippitt, ed., *Nietzsche's Futures* (Basingstoke, 1998), 167–88.

70. Nietzsche, *The Joyous Science,* aphorism 109; *Dawn of Morning,* aphorism 541. The translations are my own, but the references to works available in English will be to the aphorism number, so that the passages can be found in any edition.

71. Nietzsche, *Sämtliche Werke: Kritische Studienausgabe* (Munich, 1980), 9:11[35, 125, 207, 210] (1881).

72. Nietzsche, *Beyond Good and Evil,* aphorism 231. Nishitani Keiji, *The Self-Overcoming of Nihilism,* trans. Graham Parkes with Setsuko Aihara (Albany, 1990), 91–92.

73. Nietzsche, *Kritische Studienausgabe,* 8:11[11] and 28[6]; *Miscellaneous Opinions and Aphorisms (Human, All-too-human, vol. 2/1),* aphorism 49; *Ecce Homo,* "Why I write such good books," "Thus spoke Zarathustra," sec. 1.

74. Nietzsche, letter to Elisabeth Förster, 20 December 1885.

75. Hisamatsu Shin'ichi, *Zen and the Fine Arts* (Tokyo, 1971), 88. This interpretation of the garden at Ryōanji in terms of Hisamatsu's "seven characteristics" of Zen aesthetics is somewhat dry.

76. The following discussion is inspired by Ōhashi Ryōsuke's treatment of the aesthetic implications of the cut-continuance in his book *Kire no kōzō: Nihonbi to gendai sekai* (Structures of the cut: The beautiful in Japan and the contemporary world) (Tokyo, 1986). There is an excellent German translation by Rolf Elberfeld, *Kire: Das Schöne in Japan* (Cologne, 1994), which is an expanded edition furnished with fine photographs. For a brief account of the idea of "cuttings," see Ōhashi's essay "Kire and Iki," in Michael Kelly, ed., *The Encyclopedia of Aesthetics* (Oxford, 1998), 2:553–55.

77. Nishitani Keiji, "The Japanese Art of Arranged Flowers," trans. Jeff Shore, in Robert C. Solomon and Kathleen M. Higgins, eds, *World Philosophy: A Text with Readings* (New York, 1995), 23–27.

78. Nishitani Keiji, *Religion and Nothingness,* 137–40 and 157–59. Ōhashi discusses the rock garden at Ryōanji in terms of "likeness" in chapter two of *Kire no kōzō,* as well as Musō's use of the kanji for "temporary."

79. Dōgen, "Zazenshi" (The point of zazen).

80. Nishitani Keiji, as recounted by Robert Carter in his *Becoming Bamboo: Western and Eastern Explorations of the Meaning of Life* (Montreal and Kingston, 1992), 95.

81. Qingyuan Weixin, *Wudeng huiyuan* (Five Lamps Merged into Source), chapter 17.

82. Dietrich Seckel, *Einführung in die Kunst Ostasiens* (Munich, 1960), 360.

83. For a more detailed discussion, see my essay "Voices of Mountains, Trees, and Rivers: Kūkai, Dōgen, and a Deeper Ecology," in Mary Evelyn Tucker and Duncan Ryūken Williams, eds., *Buddhism and Ecology: The Interconnection between Dharma and Deeds* (Cambridge, Mass., 1997), 111–28.

84. Kūkai, "The Difference between Exoteric and Esoteric Buddhism," and "Attaining Enlightenment in This Very Existence," in *Kūkai: Major Works.*

85. For a fine explication of this idea, see Thomas P. Kasulis, "Reality as Embodiment: An Analysis of Kūkai's *Sokushinjōbutsu* and *Hosshin Seppō,*" in Jane Marie Law, ed., *Religious Reflections on the Human Body* (Bloomington, 1995), 166–85.

86. Kūkai, "Shōrai mokuroku," in *Major Works,* 145.

87. Dōgen, "Keisei-sanshiki."

88. Dōgen, "Busshō" (Buddha-nature); "Sangai-yuishin" (The triple world is mind only).

89. Dōgen, "Mujō-seppō"; "Keisei-sanshiki."

90. *Kūkai: Major Works,* 91.

91. Dōgen, "Jishō zammai" (The samādhi of self-enlightenment).

92. See James Hillman's eloquent essay, "In the Gardens—A Psychological Memoir," in *Consciousness and Reality: Studies in Memory of Toshihiko Izutsu* (Tokyo, 1998), 175–82. For a corresponding philosophical (but also psychological) treatment of the garden, see chapter 6 of Edward S. Casey, *Getting Back into Place: Toward a Renewed Understanding of the Place-World* (Bloomington, 1993), esp. 153–72.

93. See James Heisig's sagacious reflections on this dictum in his essays "Towards a Principle of Sufficiency," *Zen Buddhism Today* 8 (1990): 152–64.

94. Nishitani writes of the "double exposure" of the life and death perspectives in *Religion and Nothingness,* 50–53. For more on this topic see my essay, "Death and Detachment: Montaigne, Zen, Heidegger, and the Rest," in Jeff Malpas and Robert C. Solomon, eds., *Death and Philosophy* (London: Routledge, 1998), 164–80.

# SELECTED BIBLIOGRAPHY

Benl, Oscar, and Horst Hammitzsch, eds. *Japanische Geisteswelt: Vom Mythus zur Gegenwart.* Baden-Baden, 1956.

Callicott, J. Baird, and Roger T. Ames, eds. *Nature in Asian Traditions of Thought.* Albany, 1989.

Dōgen. *Shōbōgenzō.* In Ōkubo Dōshō, ed. *Dōgen zenji zenshū.* Vol. 1. Tokyo, 1969–70.

*Master Dogen's Shobogenzo.* 4 vols. Trans. Nishijima and Cross. Woking (Surrey), 1994–99.

Hay, John. *Kernels of Energy, Bones of Earth: The Rock in Chinese Art.* New York, 1985.

Hennig, Karl. *Der Karesansui-Garten als Ausdruck der Kultur der Muromachi-Zeit.* Hamburg, 1982.

Hisamatsu Shin'ichi. *Zen and the Fine Arts.* Tokyo, 1971.

Itoh Teiji. *The Gardens of Japan.* Tokyo and New York, 1984.

Ji Cheng. *The Craft of Gardens.* Trans. Alison Hardie. New Haven and London, 1988.

Jullien, François. *The Propensity of Things: Toward a History of Efficacy in China.* Trans. Janet Lloyd. New York, 1995.

Kawabata Yasunari. *Beauty and Sadness.* Trans. Howard Hibbett. Rutland and Tokyo, 1975.

Keswick, Maggie. *The Chinese Garden: History, Art & Architecture.* New York, 1978.

Kuck, Loraine. *The World of the Japanese Garden: From Chinese Origins to Modern Landscape Art.* New York and Tokyo, 1968.

Kuitert, Wybe. *Themes, Scenes, and Taste in the History of Japanese Garden Art.* Amsterdam, 1988.

*Kūkai: Major Works.* Trans. Yoshito S. Hakeda. New York, 1972.

Mori Osamu. *"Sakuteiki" no sekai: Heiancho no teienbi.* Tokyo, 1986.

Nishitani Keiji. *Religion and Nothingness.* Trans. Jan Van Bragt. Berkeley, 1982.

Ōhashi Ryōsuke. *Kire. Das Schöne in Japan.* Trans. Rolf Elberfeld. Cologne, 1994. Originally published as *Kire no kōzō: Nihonbi to gendai sekai.* Tokyo, 1986.

Parkes, Graham. "Voices of Mountains, Trees, and Rivers: Kūkai, Dōgen, and a Deeper Ecology." In Mary Evelyn Tucker and Duncan Ryūken Williams, eds. *Buddhism and Ecology: The Interconnection between Dharma and Deeds.* Cambridge, Mass., 1997.

Rambach, Pierre, and Suzanne Rambach. *Gardens of Longevity in China and Japan: The Art of the Stone Raisers.* Trans. André Marling. New York, 1987.

Schaarschmidt-Richter, Irmtraud. *Japanese Gardens.* Trans. Janet Seligman. New York, 1979.

Schafer, Edward H. *Tu Wan's Stone Catalogue of Cloudy Forest.* Berkeley, 1961.

Shigemaru Shimoyama, trans. *Sakuteiki: The Book of [the] Garden.* Tokyo, 1976.

Slawson, David A. *Secret Teachings in the Art of Japanese Gardens.* Tokyo and New York, 1987.

Stein, Rolf A. *The World in Miniature: Container Gardens and Dwellings in Far Eastern Religious Thought.* Trans. Phyllis Brooks. Stanford, 1990.

Tsunoda Ryusaku et al., eds. *Sources of Japanese Tradition.* New York and London, 1964.

# INDEX